The Huron-Wendat Feast of the Dead

WITNESS TO HISTORY

Peter Charles Hoffer and Williamjames Hull Hoffer, *Series Editors*

ALSO IN THE SERIES:

Williamjames Hull Hoffer, *The Caning of Charles Sumner: Honor, Idealism, and the Origins of the Civil War*

Tim Lehman, *Bloodshed at Little Bighorn: Sitting Bull, Custer, and the Destinies of Nations*

Daniel R. Mandell, *King Philip's War: Colonial Expansion, Native Resistance, and the End of Indian Sovereignty*

THE HURON-WENDAT FEAST OF THE DEAD

Indian–European Encounters in Early North America

ERIK R. SEEMAN

The Johns Hopkins University Press | *Baltimore*

The Johns Hopkins University Press
2715 North Charles Street
Baltimore, Maryland 21218-4363
www.press.jhu.edu

Library of Congress Cataloging-in-Publication Data
Seeman, Erik R.
    The Huron-Wendat feast of the dead : Indian-European encounters in
early North America / Erik R. Seeman.
        p.   cm. — (Witness to history)
    Includes bibliographical references and index.
    ISBN-13: 978-0-8018-9854-9 (hardcover : alk. paper)
    ISBN-10: 0-8018-9854-4 (hardcover : alk. paper)
    ISBN-13: 978-0-8018-9855-6 (pbk. : alk. paper)
    ISBN-10: 0-8018-9855-2 (pbk. : alk. paper)
    1. Wyandot Indians—Funeral customs and rites—Ontario—History—
17th century. 2. Wyandot Indians—Ontario—Social life and customs—17th
century. 3. Indians of North America—First contact with Europeans—
Ontario. 4. Jesuits—Ontario—History—17th century. I. Title.
    E99.H9S44 2011
    971.3004'97—dc22
    2010022273

A catalog record for this book is available from the British Library.

Special discounts are available for bulk purchases of this book.
For more information, please contact Special Sales at 410-516-6936 or
specialsales@press.jhu.edu.

The Johns Hopkins University Press uses environmentally friendly book
materials, including recycled text paper that is composed of at least 30
percent post-consumer waste, whenever possible. All of our book papers
are acid-free, and our jackets and covers are printed on paper with recycled
content.

CONTENTS

The Huron-Wendat Feast of the Dead

Prologue
Encounters with Bones and Death

ON MAY 12, 1636, two thousand Wendat (Huron) Indians stood on the edge of an enormous burial pit. Near the village of Ossossané in what is today Ontario, Canada, they held in their arms the bones of roughly seven hundred deceased friends and family members. The Wendats had lovingly scraped and cleaned the bones of corpses that had decomposed on scaffolds. They awaited only the signal from the master of the ritual to place the bones into the pit. This was the great Feast of the Dead.

Also standing near the burial pit was a French Catholic missionary named Jean de Brébeuf. One might assume that he was horrified by this non-Christian ritual with its unfamiliar cries and chants, and by the earlier preparation of the corpses, some only partially decomposed and seething with maggots. Yet not only was Brébeuf fascinated by the Feast of the Dead, but he also "admired" this "magnificent" ritual. He described it in great detail for French readers, telling them that it was "heartening to see" the Wendats show such devotion to their dead.[1]

Brébeuf's largely sympathetic portrayal of the Feast of the Dead drew on parallel Catholic and Wendat understandings of death and human remains.

Both groups adhered to religions that focused on the mysteries of death and the afterlife. Both believed that a dead person's soul traveled to the afterlife. Both believed that careful corpse preparation and elaborate mortuary rituals helped ensure the safe transit of the soul to the supernatural realm. And both believed in the power of human bones.

Today, when most North Americans consider human bones, we think in terms structured by modern science. Bones as deposits of calcium and other minerals surrounding living tissue. The 206 bones of the adult human skeleton. The site of the production of red blood cells. Cranium, coccyx, clavicle.

Four hundred years ago, when Wendats and French Catholics met in North America, their associations with human bones differed greatly from our own—but closely resembled one another's. Bones to heal the sick and to tie together far-flung villages. Bones invested with supernatural power. The site of connection between this world and another world. Community, curing, condolence.

These similarities, and other death-related ones, helped facilitate communication between Wendats and the French. Even though the two groups spoke different languages, they shared a common tongue based on the veneration of human remains and the centrality of mortuary practices.

Building on this insight, it is possible to use the Feast of the Dead—or more precisely, the meeting of Wendats and Frenchmen on the edge of the Ossossané burial pit in 1636—as a metaphor for Indian-European encounters in North America. When native peoples met Europeans in the sixteenth and seventeenth centuries, parallel customs, and especially parallel mortuary practices, allowed for understanding across cultural boundaries. When each side saw the other performing funerals, they realized that their counterparts were neither gods nor demons but humans like themselves. Because both indigenous peoples and Europeans placed so much weight on proper burials, they were curious about the other's practices. And tragically, because the encounter caused countless deaths due to warfare and epidemics, both groups had numerous opportunities to witness the other's funeral practices. Indeed, many of the Wendats buried in Ossossané (pronounced uh-SOSS-uh-nee) had succumbed to European diseases.

As a result of these parallel practices, the French and Wendats often communicated with one another in the language of *deathways*, a term that encompasses deathbed scenes, burial practices, funerals, mourning rituals, and commemoration of the dead. Yet cross-cultural communication could be put to manipulative as well as constructive ends. In the frequently adversarial context of the European colonization of North America, knowledge was a precious commodity that could be used against one's enemies. It did not take long before this dynamic emerged in French-Wendat relations.

Using the Feast of the Dead as a metaphor also highlights the specifically *spiritual* component of Indian-European encounters in North America. Students have long been taught that Europeans came to the New World for gold, glory, and God. Many students, however, are more impressed by the first two motivations than the third. In classrooms they frequently voice the opinion that Europeans' desire for riches and renown greatly outweighed their interest in spreading the word of Christ. Even when Europeans professed a commitment to teaching natives about Christianity, these classroom skeptics assert, this merely disguised their more powerful desires for material wealth and personal acclaim.

These students' arguments are not without merit; many professional historians have made similar points. Bruce Trigger, for example, emphasized material over spiritual motivations among both Wendats and the French in his landmark *The Children of Aataentsic: A History of the Huron People to 1660*. Trigger, an archaeologist and historian so respected by native peoples that he was adopted as an honorary member of the Huron-Wendat Nation, was too careful of a scholar to argue that religious beliefs were entirely unimportant in the interactions between Wendats and the French. But he did consistently place the desire for goods over the desire for spiritual fulfillment. He asserted that the French interest in colonizing Canada was primarily about profiting from the valuable fur trade, and he likewise insisted that Wendat interest in Christianity was mostly instrumental, that is, a means to an end. According to Trigger, Wendats who accepted the missionaries' teachings did so in large part to gain access to European trade goods such as copper kettles and iron knives, which helped make daily life easier and promised greater success in warfare.

My interpretation, building on recent histories of other encounters between American Indians and Europeans, inverts Trigger's formulation. Yes, Wendats were interested in European metalware, and yes, they sought these goods because they promised greater convenience and fighting power than their native-made counterparts. But also important were the items' religious implications. For the Wendats, material objects possessed spiritual power. This was expressed most clearly in deathways, as the bereaved gave the dead gifts to be brought to the afterlife, and they offered presents to friends and ritual specialists as tokens of the reciprocal ties that bound a community together. Newly available European goods quickly became central to Wendat mortuary practices, including the Feast of the Dead. In the Ossossané burial pit, Wendats carefully placed European glass beads and copper kettles alongside the remains of their loved ones.

Even beyond the connection with spiritually powerful trade items that frequently ended up as grave goods, many individuals involved in the encounter were motivated primarily by religious goals. French missionaries such as Jean de Brébeuf believed that baptism saved Wendat souls from eternal damnation. And some Wendats, in a time of rapid change brought on by an influx of European goods and pathogens, found themselves open to new interactions with the supernatural world.

Like Trigger's interpretation, mine is based on sources that leave much to be desired. Most problematically, one finds written evidence of seventeenth-century Wendat perceptions only in works authored by Europeans. French explorers such as Samuel de Champlain and missionaries such as Gabriel Sagard penned books about the Wendats and their customs. Even more abundant sources appear in the *Jesuit Relations*, accounts written by the Jesuit order of Catholic missionaries in Canada. Jesuits wrote these *Relations* intermittently starting in 1611 and then published them annually between 1632 and 1673.

The *Relations* were largely fundraising tools: aimed at pious Catholics in France, they were intended to spur readers to open their pocketbooks in support of Jesuit missionary efforts. One may reasonably ask whether this context caused the authors of the *Relations* to exaggerate their successes or failures. It seems that this was not the case. The fundraising context of the *Relations* pulled the Jesuits in opposing directions. The missionaries did not want to seem too successful, or readers might think contributions were unnecessary. Nor did the Jesuits want to seem like abject failures, lest potential donors resist throwing good money after bad. Ultimately it seems that the Jesuits had an incentive to portray their efforts relatively realistically, narrating both triumphs and disappointments.

More difficult to explain away is how the written sources were embedded in European ways of seeing the world. While most French authors worked hard to accurately describe the Wendats and other native groups, they did so using European frames of reference. Sometimes this led to relatively innocuous metaphors and comparisons, as when Sagard described dog meat, a Wendat delicacy, as having "a taste rather like pork."[2] Other times this European perspective had more serious consequences, as when missionaries insisted that the Wendat reverence for *okis* or spirits was in fact devil worship, an interpretation that led Jesuits to try to prevent rituals for communicating with the *okis*.

Even the most basic matter of naming these people is shaped by European biases in the written sources. The indigenous people who are the subject of this book called themselves (and still call themselves) Wendats, yet for four centuries most Euro-Americans have referred to them as "Hurons," following the practice of the earliest Europeans who wrote about them. The word "huron" was an Old French epithet meaning "rustic" or "ruffian"; a modern English analogue might be "hillbilly" or "hick." In this and other ways the surviving written perspective on the Wendat-French encounter inevitably distorts aspects of native society that Europeans overlooked, did not understand, or were downright contemptuous about.

Yet another, underused body of sources on Indian-European encounters remains. Archaeology, although not without its own biases and shortcomings, allows us to corroborate, complement, and sometimes counter European descriptions with the excavated remains of the past. It also allows us to understand some characteristics of Wendat society in the centuries before Europeans arrived. These material sources are especially valuable for understanding mortuary customs. Deathways left more traces in the physical record than many other activities, such as sexual relations and child-rearing practices. As a result, archaeology provides valuable information about Wendat deathways before and after contact with Europeans.

Still, archaeologists' modern, scientific understanding of bones—as sources of data to be measured and weighed and peered at under microscopes—would eventually cause conflict. Descendants of the Wendats and other indigenous groups began in the late twentieth century to voice more loudly their demands that their ancestors' remains be returned. This issue still vexes the museums and universities that hold indigenous human remains. The Feast of the Dead thus continues to resonate nearly four centuries after the Wendats and Brébeuf stood on the edge of the Ossossané burial pit, waiting for the signal to bury the bones.

one   The Origins of Wendake

EVERYONE HAS AN ORIGIN STORY: an account of how the world was made and how it came to be filled with humans and animals. Whether it is a secular humanist today confidently describing the big bang and survival of the fittest, a seventeenth-century Wendat elder patiently relating how the Earth emerged on the back of a turtle's shell, or a Jesuit missionary insisting that the biblical story of Adam and Eve is the only truthful account, all people feel the need to explain the mystery of how we got here. These stories make sense to those who relate them, partly because people usually don't question the underlying logic of their own stories, and partly because the narratives embody values taken for granted by the storytellers. But these accounts can seem strange to outsiders who don't share the storytellers' beliefs.

This is true for the Wendat creation story. It made perfect sense to seventeenth-century Wendats, but it struck missionaries as nonsense, as "nothing but myths."[1] Even readers today, who are more tolerant of unfamiliar belief systems than were the Jesuits, are often inclined to treat the story with condescension. But it is worth seriously grappling with the narrative, because it reveals the intimate connections between this world and the spirit world, between life and death, that were at the heart of the Wendat worldview.

The creation story, however, cannot fully reveal the origins of Wendake (wen-DAH-kee), the Wendat homeland. Because it was first recorded in the early seventeenth century, the story served the needs of the residents of Wendake at that time, and not necessarily those of the previous centuries, when the story may have differed. Although it certainly drew on earlier accounts, it does not explain how and when Wendats came to inhabit the fertile land they eventually called home. For that we must turn to archaeology. The material culture of Wendake does not supply all the answers, but combined with the origin story it provides a surprisingly vivid picture of how Wendats experienced life and death on the eve of direct contact with Europeans.

In the beginning, a female spirit named Aataentsic lived in the sky with other spirits. One day while she was working in a field, her dog began to chase a bear. Running after the two animals, she fell into a hole and plunged out of the sky toward the watery world below. The turtle that lived in the water saw Aataentsic falling and urged the other aquatic animals to gather soil from the seabed and place it on his shell. They hurriedly did as he said, quickly forming an island onto which Aataentsic gently landed. Thus the name for the storytellers' homeland (Wendake, *the island*) and for themselves (Wendats, *those who live on the island*).

Aataentsic happened to be pregnant when she fell to Earth and soon gave birth to a daughter. Eventually the daughter magically became pregnant and died giving birth to twin boys, Tawiscaron and Iouskeha. When these boys grew into men, they began to quarrel. Wielding a sharp set of deer antlers as a weapon, Iouskeha bloodied his brother and then chased him down and killed him. Tawiscaron's death was not entirely in vain, however: his fallen droplets of blood turned into flint, a crucial material out of which Wendats fashioned their axes and arrowheads.

After this, Iouskeha (representing the sun) and his grandmother Aataentsic (the moon) took up residence in the sky. They lived together much as Wendats did on Earth: in a bark longhouse surrounded by cornfields, in a land abounding in fish and game. This was the village of the dead, the land to the west of Wendake that was the destination for the souls of humans after they died. This village was the only destination for souls. Wendats did not have one afterlife for the souls of the good and another for those of the evil. They generally did not think in terms of simple binaries like good and evil: all people, and even all spirits, had elements of both. In the village of the dead Aataentsic was the one in charge of taking care of the souls. And the renewal of life provided by the spirit world was suggested by Iouskeha's immortality: every time he grew old, he was able to renew his youth and become a healthy man of twenty-five or thirty years. Likewise, the souls in the village of the dead enjoyed perpetual good harvests and fair weather.

From their home in the sky, Iouskeha and Aataentsic influenced the lives of humans. Iouskeha generally tried to make things better for the residents of Wendake. He created all the animals of the Earth, which allowed the Wendats to prosper through hunting and fishing. As the sun, he provided fine weather and warmth and protected warriors by allowing them to find their way through the woods. His grandmother, by contrast, often spoiled Iouskeha's efforts. Not only did she bring bad weather, but she also brought disease and death. Aataentsic was a spirit to be feared. For this reason, when she took on a human shape and appeared at feasts (as personified by a dancer), Wendats hurled insults at her.

This origin story illustrates several beliefs that were important to the Wendats when the narrative was first written down in the early seventeenth century. It points to the sky as the locus of Wendat spirituality. Not only did the two most powerful spirits live there, but it was also the location of the village of souls. Similarly important was that the boundary between the Earth and the spirit world was permeable. Iouskeha and Aataentsic could move between the spirit world and this world, as could the souls of the dead. And the souls of most Wendats would eventually travel to the village of souls, except for a few too old or too young to make the arduous journey. Death was not a joyful subject in the Wendat creation story, but it was a perfectly natural part of life, something that from the very creation of Earth humans could not escape. And death wasn't always a bad thing, as proven by the flint that resulted from Tawiscaron's blood, and by the blood spilled by animals who gave their lives so humans could survive. Moreover, the comfortable and familiar landscape of the village of souls made it seem like an unthreatening place.

Finally, the story—especially when told in its original language—suggests the importance of human remains in the Wendat worldview. The Wendat word for souls, used again and again in the story, is *esken*, which is closely related to the word for bones, *atisken*. According to a linguist, the meaning of the root "*sken*" is "to be a manifestation of humans after death, particularly, but not exclusively, bones."[2] As Wendats conceived it, when a person died, his or her two souls stayed with the corpse until the Feast of the Dead, at which point one soul separated from the bones and went to Aataentsic's village in the sky. The other soul remained in or near the ossuary unless it was reanimated in a newborn Wendat child. Those who listened to the Wendat creation story heard over and over this linguistic connection between bones and souls, between human remains and the spirit world.

What they did not hear was a historical account of how Wendats came to live between what we call Georgian Bay and Lake Simcoe. For although the origin story focused on the creation of the "island" of Wendake, that region had been only recently occupied by humans. Between roughly 500 and 1300 CE, there seems to have been no permanent human habitation in what came to be called Wendake. A lack of large mammals, especially deer, made the region less attractive than areas to the south. But starting around the year 1300, people who lived along the north shore of Lake Ontario, near the site of present-day Toronto, began to migrate to the northwest. They left their previous homeland in response to a recent increase in population, which put pressure on local resources. These were Iroquoian people, members of one of the two major linguistic groups of northeastern North America (the other is the Algonquian group). These people from near Lake Ontario shared beliefs, language, and material culture with Iroquoians in present-day New York, Pennsylvania, and the Niagara Frontier. The Ontario Iroquoians had long known about the area to the north and probably had visited there on hunting and fishing expeditions.

The land to which they migrated, and which they would call Wendake, was (and, for the most part, still is) a beautiful landscape of hills and forests dominated by the presence of water. Clear streams ran through Wendake, filled with trout and bass. In the lakes surrounding the "island," enormous fish such as northern pike and sturgeon provided year-round sustenance. Georgian Bay held countless whitefish, which, when spawning in the fall, ran in schools and could be caught by the hundreds. The forests abounded with small game such as rabbits and squirrels and, after trees had been cleared for agriculture, white-tailed deer, drawn to the "edge habitat" where field meets forest. And the sandy soil proved to be well suited to the "three sisters" that dominated Iroquoian agriculture: corn, beans, and squash. Of these three, corn was the centerpiece of the Wendat diet, as it could easily be dried and used year-

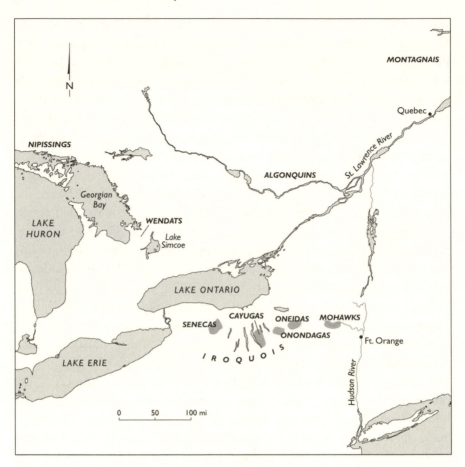

Northeastern North America. Drawn by Bill Nelson.

round. This was crucial in a land powerfully marked by the four seasons, each bearing its own color and foods to add to the staple of corn: muddy brown spring with turkeys calling for mates, green summer with plentiful turtles and frogs, orange autumn with pumpkins ripening on the vine, and white winter, difficult to be sure, but also an opportunity to catch fish through the ice and to hunt deer struggling through the crusty snow.

This fertile landscape attracted numerous immigrants and allowed the residents of Wendake to quickly increase their numbers. Long before Columbus and other Europeans came to the New World, Wendat society was dynamic and changing. In 1330 the Wendats numbered about 750 and occupied two villages. A generation later three thousand Wendats lived in nine villages. Immigration slowed thereafter, but natural increase remained strong through the fifteenth century. By 1500 the Wendats numbered about twenty-one thousand, grouped into four nations: the Bear People, the Rock People, the Deer People, and the Cord-Making People.[3] After this their numbers leveled off, with births and deaths in roughly equal numbers, as the population density came close to what the region's natural resources could sustain.

At some point in the sixteenth century, the dozen or so villages of the Bear People joined with the four villages of the Cord-Making People to form the Wendat Confederacy. Early in the seventeenth century, the smaller Deer Nation and Rock Nation joined their neighbors in the confederacy. Like the more famous Five Nations of Iroquois to the south, the Wendat Confederacy seems to have been inspired by strategic considerations. The culturally and linguistically linked Wendat nations stood in a better position to defend themselves against enemies if they joined together.

Their union also allowed them to prosper in trade with other native peoples by avoiding undue intra-Wendat competition. Located about as far north as corn agriculture could survive, Wendake became known among the native peoples of northeastern North America as a clearinghouse of trade. Hunter-gatherers from the north brought their plush pelts of beaver, marten, and arctic fox to the Wendats to exchange for dried corn that would help them survive lean periods. Agriculturalists from the south brought tobacco and exotic shells to Wendake, hoping to get their hands on the warm northern furs. But despite their trading acumen, Wendats did not pursue profit in a strict economic sense. Yes, they hoped to gain necessities and luxuries, many of which wound up in their burials. But exchange served another vitally important function as well: amicable trade was the foundation of peaceable relations with foreigners. The Wendats' goal was not simply to get the best "price" for their corn in furs or tobacco, but to maintain communication and reciprocal ties with their neighbors.

By the early seventeenth century, then, the four nations of the Wendat Confederacy were a powerful force in the region. They occupied twenty-five villages of roughly 500 to 1,500 individuals each. A typical village covered about 2 acres within a defensive palisade and was surrounded by many more acres of cornfields, but some smaller villages did not have palisades. Although men cleared the farming fields, women were the primary agricultural workers. They were in charge of loosening the soil with hoes, planting seeds, pull-

ing weeds, and harvesting crops—not to mention preparing and cooking all
the food that resulted from their efforts, especially *sagamité*, the corn porridge that was the foundation of the Wendat diet. This all was hard work, but
women gained power and recognition from their role as providers. This was
mirrored by the fact that the Wendats were matrilineal (they traced kinship
through the female line) and matrilocal (when a couple married the man
moved in with the woman's family).

A man joining a woman in her home entered the female-dominated
space of the longhouse. Most Wendat villages contained about two dozen
longhouses. These characteristically Iroquoian structures are aptly named:
the typical longhouse measured 150 feet in length, and archaeologists have
found evidence of several nearly 250 feet long. Inside the average longhouse
eight or ten families lived, not all mixed together, but each family with its
own sleeping area and a hearth they shared with one other family. In these
close quarters—especially during the long winter—Wendat women and men
shared stories such as the origin narrative. Elders taught the younger generation what it meant to live and die a Wendat.

Many of the stories they told revolved around the relationship between
the visible world and the spirit world. For Wendats, these two realms were
intimately connected. What happened in the visible world was influenced
by spirits, which could travel back and forth from their world to the world of
humans and animals. Wendats told stories about how certain human spirits
or souls had wandered abroad and seen the village of the dead.

But humans were not the only creatures with souls: animals had them too.
This powerfully influenced Wendat hunting and fishing practices. Because
each animal or fish they killed for subsistence had a soul, Wendats needed to
perform rituals before the hunt and especially after the creature was dead. If
not, the unhappy spirit of the dead animal would return to this world angry,
and it would tell the spirits of other animals not to cooperate with the Wendat
hunters and fishermen. The rituals revolved around the respectful treatment
of animal bones, because that was where souls resided. Wendats never threw
animal bones into the cooking fire or tossed them to their dogs; to do so
would be to show the greatest disrespect for the animal spirits.

In addition to believing that humans and animals had souls, Wendats believed that nonliving things such as rocks and rivers did too. The distinctions
we make today between animate and inanimate objects did not hold sway
for Wendats. It is unclear whether they believed that every single nonliving

object had a spirit: every grain of sand, every snowflake. But they certainly held that large, powerful, or otherwise unusual inanimate objects had spirits. If a Wendat traveling through the forest found a stone shaped like a spoon or a pot, he was likely to keep it as a charm. This, he believed, had been lost by a spirit who lived in the forest, and the item itself had a soul that would allow its bearer to connect with the spirit world. Awe-inspiring natural phenomena such as waterfalls or rapids also had spirits, which sometimes needed to be placated with an offering of tobacco in order to ensure a safe journey. Several hundred miles away from Wendake there stood a remarkable rock formation. It looked like a human with two arms raised; Wendats said a man had been turned to stone when standing in that posture. When Wendats passed this figure on their long-distance trading journeys, they threw some tobacco to the rock, saying, "Here, take courage, and let us have a good journey."[4]

But the spirits that Wendats most fervently worshipped were those of the sky and sun. Wendats personified the sun as Iouskeha, grandson of Aataentsic, and he brought warmth and comfort to the people of Wendake. The sky seems not to have been personified in a similar way. Rather, the sky spirit remained more mysterious, and more fickle, than Iouskeha. The sky spirit could heal the sick; thus, when someone was ill, that person would throw some tobacco into the fire and say, "O Sky, here is what I offer you in sacrifice; have pity on me, assist me, heal me." Because the sky spirit was omnipresent, Wendats sealed their oaths by invoking it. If someone made a promise, she would seal it by saying, "The sky knows what we are doing today," implying that to go back on the promise would anger the sky spirit, which had witnessed the oath.[5] When the sky spirit was angry, it could bring bad weather, ruin crops, or even cause people to drown or freeze to death.

Although praying to spirits such as the sky spirit could be an effective way of gaining their favor, the most common way for humans to communicate with the spirit world was through dreams. Wendats believed that the human soul was not fixed inside its bodily container; rather, the soul could leave the body, usually at night during sleep, and temporarily enter the spirit world. When the soul returned to the body, it communicated its experiences in the spirit world to the dreamer. When the person awoke, he or she needed to figure out what the dream meant and how to proceed. Sometimes this was clear, while other times it required the mediation of a shaman.

It is difficult to overstate how much importance Wendats placed on these nocturnal communications with the spirit world. Once, a man awoke in the middle of the night having just dreamed that the spirits wanted him to throw a feast for his neighbors. He immediately went to work getting the feast in order, waking others in the village so he could borrow a kettle. Other times a person would dream that he or she needed to obtain an unusual object belonging to someone else: a charm the person had found in the forest, or a well-made spear. The dreamer would then inform the owner of the object about the dream, and the person with the charm or spear would (usually) willingly give it to the one who had the dream.

Moreover, a dream could influence the fate of an entire village. If a leading warrior had a dream that his people needed to attack a far-off enemy, young men soon started applying war paint. If a well-respected elder had a dream that the village must throw an eat-all feast—an event that could last for days and involve the consumption of enormous quantities of food—women quickly set kettles atop their fires and readied dogs and deer to be boiled. These last two examples point to the fact that not all dreamers were accorded the same respect. Dreams of highly respected men and women could send a village into a bustle of activity, while the dreams of more marginal individuals might be disregarded.

The danger of ignoring dreams, however, was that doing so could anger the soul that had brought the message from the spirit world. An angry soul manifested its displeasure by causing the sickness or even death of its associated human. For this reason, dreaming and healing were tightly intertwined. Wendats were a relatively healthy people, with a low-fat diet and high-exercise lifestyle that would be the envy of many today. Yet as with all preindustrial peoples, Wendats had a much shorter life expectancy than residents of the modern industrialized world. This was largely due to high rates of infant mortality. Roughly 120 to 180 out of every 1,000 Wendat children born did not survive their first year. This compares with an infant mortality rate in the United States today of only 7 per 1,000. Infants died from respiratory infections that turned into pneumonia and from malnutrition during Wendake's long winter.

Older children, however, suffered less sickness than their European counterparts, because the Americas were home to no epidemic infectious diseases before the arrival of Europeans. Owing to the New World's low population density, infectious diseases such as smallpox and influenza simply did not evolve, as there were not enough potential hosts to keep the viruses alive. Moreover, American Indians' lack of domesticated animals also worked against the transmission of animal diseases to humans. Scientists believe, for example, that measles jumped from dogs to humans in Europe and that leprosy was transmitted from water buffaloes in Asia.

As a result of this lack of contagious diseases, 70 percent of Wendat children lived to the age of fifteen, compared to only 50 percent of European children. Wendats who made it to adulthood could expect to live on average to about fifty years old. Adult Wendats sometimes died from diseases present in the New World such as tuberculosis, but more frequently from accidents that occurred while hunting or cooking, environmental hazards such as smoky longhouses that induced respiratory illnesses, malnutrition during periods of scarcity, and warfare.

Some sicknesses Wendats thought had natural, as opposed to supernatural, causes: a woman burned herself cooking, for example, and the injury began to fester. For these natural problems Wendats had natural remedies. The burned woman might make a tea out of various healing herbs, or she might apply a poultice of wild roots to the injured area, or if it got really bad someone might use a sharp stone to make an incision into the wound to release the corruption and excess blood. Other natural illnesses might be treated with herbs that acted as emetics, or with burning brands to cause scarification.

But Wendats believed that most illnesses resulted from supernatural causes, usually because the soul's desires had not been adequately met and the angry soul had allowed a sickness spirit to attack the person. These cases required supernatural remedies. The first step was for the sick person to summon a healer. The healer, who seems always to have been a man, gained his power through apprenticeship and vision quests, although nothing was more important than developing a reputation for effectiveness by successfully curing the sick. Healers were often physically out of the ordinary, either handicapped in some way (blind, or severely hunchbacked) or marked by dwarfism. Wendats believed that these were physical manifestations of spiritual power. Indeed, the Wendat word for healers was *oki*, which meant powerful spirit, and which the French often translated as "demon." Because of their ability to contact and influence the spirit world, as well as their association with life and death, healers were some of the most powerful, revered, and even feared individuals in Wendake.

When the healer visited a sick person, he first attempted to discern why the person's soul was angry. What hidden desires of the soul had been neglected? To determine this, the healer would employ a variety of methods. He might peer into a basin of water, and if he saw reflected in the surface of the water an object such as a fine beaded collar or a robe of highly esteemed black squirrel skins, the healer would indicate that this was what the soul wanted. Or he might gaze into a fire while shaking a turtle rattle, again looking for the shape of coveted objects to appear. Or he might isolate himself in a sweat lodge and, amid the heat and darkness, see the cause of the problem. More difficult cases might require the healer to fast for a number of days to induce a vision that would reveal the desires of the sick person's soul.

If all the soul required was an object, then every effort would be made to bring it to the sick person. But more often, what the soul needed was a feast. Wendats held feasts for a variety of reasons, but one of the most important was to heal the body and soul of the afflicted. Wendats believed that feasts helped to assuage an angry soul by offering it lavish food and gifts, while the sickness demon could be scared away by the noise of dancing and singing. Feasts were also impressive displays of community togetherness, as an entire village would typically be mobilized to throw an elaborate feast.

In one case, a woman lay gravely ill and it was determined that her soul needed a feast with a performance by fifty dancers. It took the villagers three days to get ready for the great event, preparing food, mending costumes, and making drums and rattles. On the morning of the feast, the village elders gathered to announce that the time had come for the dancers to wash themselves. Later, the elders declared that now they must grease their bodies. Two more announcements followed, indicating when the dancers should put on their costumes and their beads. Finally, as anticipation built throughout the village, the elders said that the feast was about to begin and all should attend. As many as humanly possible squeezed into the sick woman's longhouse, where she lay in the center. The male and female dancers entered the longhouse, led by a pair who continually shook a turtle rattle and served as the masters of the ceremony.

The masters of the dance took their places near the patient, one at her head and one at her feet, shaking the turtle rattle and chanting. Around them wheeled the fifty other dancers, singing louder and louder, all attentive to their crucial role in helping this woman recover, all trying to scare away the sickness demon with their noise. One can imagine the intensity of this scene from the patient's perspective as she lay in the longhouse, surrounded by whirling dancers lit by the cabin's smoky fires, their shadows in distorted shapes on the walls, their songs filling the dwelling with spiritual power.

Healing Ceremony. The artist based this image on a description written by Samuel de Champlain. Ceremonies like this were ordinarily held indoors, but otherwise the artist's representation seems fairly accurate. The leader of the dance carries a turtle rattle, a key component of the shaman's arsenal. The assembled Wendats watch the proceedings with rapt attention. From Champlain, *Voyages et descouvertures* (1619). Courtesy of the Library of Congress.

One might think that the patient was grateful for all this attention, but in this case she was not. Healing ceremonies could reflect village unity, but they could also reflect tensions between what the patient expected and what actually happened. In the end, many healing feasts were simply unsuccessful. In this instance the sick woman complained that the dancers had forgotten several crucial parts of the ritual. She also said that the ceremony did not make her feel any better, so five or six days later she went to a nearby village for another healing feast, but it was to no avail and she died.[6]

Despite the best efforts of dream interpreters, healers, and dancers, they often could not prevent death. When it became clear that a sick person would not recover, Wendats mobilized their rituals of dying and death. First and foremost, Wendats expected the dying to show no fear of death. Unlike today, when people visiting the mortally ill usually try to avoid the subject of death, Wendats openly talked with the dying person about the impending funeral. Family members showed the dying person the robes and moccasins in which she would be buried and asked her to choose the items she wanted placed onto her burial scaffold with her.

A stoic demeanor was especially important for those warriors who were captured and tortured to death by rival native groups. Both the Wendats and their Iroquois enemies engaged in warfare largely to garner captives rather than to inflict large losses of life. Some of these captives were adopted by families that had lost members to warfare or disease, whereas others were ritually tortured to death. Wendats aimed to stretch out the captive's agony as long as possible, starting with the extremities and working toward the vital organs over the course of one, two, or even three days. The prisoner did his best to show no fear of death, singing his war song or mocking his torturers despite unimaginable pain. If the prisoner was especially courageous in dying, the captors would eat his heart so as to gain his bravery. The captors would also sometimes cut incisions in the upper part of their necks and allow some of the dead man's blood to mingle with their own, again to gain his power. Even if the prisoner was weak and cried out, ritual cannibalism marked the final triumph of the victors over the prisoner.

Outside of the context of war, those who did not die unexpectedly customarily held an *athataion* or farewell feast, another opportunity to display courage in the face of death. It is unclear whether the farewell feast was a ritual performed only for males. No description of the *athataion* explicitly states that it was sex-specific, yet all the examples we have are farewell feasts for men and boys. Whatever the case, the whole village was invited to this event, in which food played a central role. The literal meaning of *athataion* was "one makes his last meal."[7] Women therefore prepared copious amounts of fish, venison, and *sagamité* for the guests, with the dying man receiving the choicest portions of food. Thus fortified, he addressed the assembled crowd, telling them that he did not fear death, indeed that he looked forward to the afterlife. His words were accorded great respect and attention: these were the words of someone about to enter the spirit world. If he was a warrior, he would jauntily sing his war song. His family members and friends matched his buoyant mood. There were no tears at a farewell feast, only good food and shared memories of a life well lived.

The mood changed dramatically when the person died. Women, girls, and boys began to wail and groan, filling the longhouse with their lamentations. Adult men did not weep; instead, they adopted the conventional Wendat posture of grief, with a serious look on their faces and their heads sunk upon their knees. But the others more than made up for the men's silence. The mourners worked themselves into a passion by remembering others who had died, crying out, "And my father is dead, and my mother is dead, and my cousin is dead," and so on through all their deceased relatives. Finally, after enough collective anguish had been expressed, an elder called out, "It's enough, stop weeping!" and the lamentations ceased.[8] Family members readied the body for burial by flexing it tightly in the fetal position, wrapping it in the person's finest beaver robe, and laying it on its side on a reed mat, where it would remain for the roughly three days of preparation for the funeral.

Messengers now sprinted to nearby villages to spread the word about the death. The runners invited far-flung friends and family members to yet another feast, this called the *agochin atiskein* or feast of the souls (not to be confused with the Feast of the Dead). While the messengers were abroad, elders called out, "All take courage, and prepare the best feast you can, for such a one who has died!"[9] The farewell feast had been lavish, but it paled alongside the abundance of the feast of the souls—especially if the deceased had been a respected elder or widely known warrior. The Wendats did not have dramatic differences in rank and status between the highest and lowest members of society, but there were people held in especially high esteem on account of their spiritual power or martial exploits. At the feast of the souls for such individuals, kettles overflowed with deer, and bowls could barely hold delicacies such as *sagamité* flavored with fermented fish.

But even less-renowned Wendats had rousing feasts of souls thrown in their honor. This was because Wendats believed that the soul of the deceased took part in the feast, enjoying one last great banquet and gaining sustenance for the arduous journey to the village of the dead. Of equal importance were the speeches. One after the other, elders stood up and consoled the survivors, saying, "there was no longer any remedy, he must indeed die, we are all subject to death."[10] The elders also comforted the bereaved with stories of the deceased's good-heartedness, generosity, patience, and—if he had been a warrior—his courage.

Ordinarily, this was the point at which the corpse would be carried to the village cemetery for burial on a scaffold. But there were certain unusual circumstances for which Wendats reserved atypical burial practices. A baby less than a month or two old was buried by a pathway, so its soul could rise up and enter the womb of a young woman to be born again. A more elaborate procedure awaited those who died by drowning or freezing to death, because Wendats believed that this was caused by the sky spirit's anger. As a result, extraordinary means were necessary to appease the sky: the dead person's flesh must be consumed by fire, perhaps to more readily sacrifice it to the sky in the form of smoke. In the cemetery the corpse was laid on the ground, a pit to one side and a fire to the other. Young men wielding knives cut away the fleshiest parts of the body and then opened the abdomen and removed the entrails. The men placed the flesh and guts into the fire and then buried the remainder of the corpse in the earth.

But for the vast majority of Wendats, scaffold burial was the method of primary interment, or first burial. With the feast of the souls complete and the kettles emptied, an elder announced that the body was about to be carried to the cemetery, which lay a few hundred yards outside the village palisade. Cemeteries were considered the most sacred sites in all of Wendake; if a village caught fire, residents would rush out and save the corpses before they worried about their longhouses and belongings. So it was with great solemnity that four men placed the corpse onto a litter or stretcher made of wooden poles and reed matting and then covered the body with another beaver robe. These men carried the body to the cemetery as the whole village followed them in a silent and somber procession. They placed the litter next to a scaffold that had been prepared, with four wooden poles and a platform made out of bark. The scaffold stood 8 to 10 feet above ground to prevent animals from gnawing at the corpse.

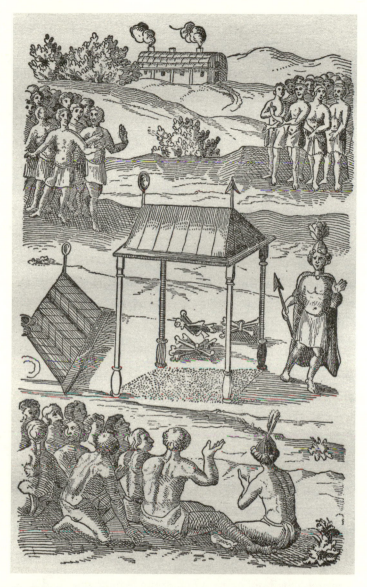

Scaffold Burial. This was the ordinary method of Wendat primary interment. Again the artist takes liberties where Champlain's descriptions are wanting: the scaffold's poles and the longhouse's chimneys reflect European rather than Wendat design. But the high scaffold holding a bark tomb gives a sense of the physical dimension of Wendat burials, and the crowds of onlookers convey the social importance of funerals. From Champlain, *Voyages et descouvertures* (1619). Courtesy of the Library of Congress.

Before the body was placed on the scaffold, however, mourners brought presents: for the deceased, the bereaved, and those who officiated at the funeral. The mourners carried their presents to an elder, who was standing on a tree stump or other elevated spot. He would then announce the gifts: "Here is a necklace of shell beads that Teientoen has brought to dry the tears of Arakhié."[11] Others brought native items such as beaver robes and projectile points, or, after 1570 or so, European goods such as iron hatchets and copper kettles. These European items were obtained indirectly at first, from other indigenous peoples who had direct contact with Europeans, and after 1609 directly from the French. Wendats considered it a great honor to be able to give gifts at a funeral; indeed, this was perhaps the main reason they accumulated goods in the first place. Giving gifts at a funeral gained favor with the deceased's soul, which was about to enter the spirit world, and displayed the gift giver's generosity to the other villagers. Some of the gifts were placed with the corpse, which was then enclosed in a bark structure similar to a coffin and raised onto the scaffold, there to slowly decompose.

Returning to the village, family members now entered a period of mourning. As in many societies, Wendats divided their mourning into a brief period of deep mourning followed by a longer period of lesser mourning. The ten-day period of deep mourning was observed only by a woman for her dead husband and a man for his dead wife. During this period the bereaved remained inside the longhouse, lying face down on a mat, covered in furs. If someone came to visit, the mourner's only response would be "*cway*" or good day, and then he or she resumed silence. The bereaved ate cold food and allowed a big chunk of hair to be cut from the back of the head—an apt symbol of conjugal grief, as Wendats took great pride in their hair, and this mourning haircut made them look unattractive. After the ten days were over, mourners slowly returned to their routines, although they remained disheveled and unkempt for a year, with women sometimes blackening their faces with charcoal. Both men and women waited at least a year to remarry.

Face blackened, hair unkempt, a mourning woman returned frequently to the cemetery to weep by the scaffold that held her husband's remains. Her noisy lamentations contrasted with the silence of the bones, which quietly awaited the Feast of the Dead.

two

Catholicism and Colonization

A WOMAN AWAKENS IN THE FIRST GRAY LIGHT of morning, the silence reminding her of her husband's recent death. She pulls on some warm garments and heads to the village cemetery, where she weeps over his bodily remains.

Tables groan with food at the funeral feast of a well-respected man. Residents from all the surrounding villages have been summoned to partake in the abundance. Above the din one can barely hear the speeches extolling the dead man's valor on the battlefield.

A spiritually powerful man dies after showing no fear of death. His body is boiled so his skeleton may be easily taken apart and distributed to those who hope to be healed by the power of the holy bones.

Scenes from Wendake? No, these imagined moments are based on the beliefs and practices of people unknown to the Wendats before the sixteenth century. Thousands of miles away, French Catholics practiced a faith that differed in many important ways from Wendat religion. In particular, Catholic leaders nurtured an evangelizing impulse: a desire to spread their faith to nonbelievers that was entirely foreign to Wendat religion. Yet in their mortuary rituals and attitudes toward human remains these religions included a surprising number of similarities. Because of these parallels, when the French and Wendats met in North America, deathways were a crucial means by which the two groups communicated with one another.

French missionaries brought their religion, with its defining image of a dead or dying man on a wooden cross, to a people for whom human remains were invested with great sacred significance. They also brought the central paradoxes of Christianity—that in the death of Jesus Christ lay the promise of eternal life for all humans, and that in death humans were released from this world into an eternal afterlife—to a people with their own powerful vision of the relationship between the human and spirit worlds. And they brought their culture's belief in the omnipresence of the dead—that those in the after-life deserved the constant attention of the living, which gave the impression of the dead being everywhere—to a society that likewise maintained power-ful bonds between the dead and the living. These and other issues related to life and death became central to the interactions between Wendats and the French. It is therefore crucial to understand the religious context of New World colonization and the religious beliefs of the missionaries.

We begin by examining Catholicism in roughly 1450, before the Protestant Reformation sundered Western Europe into competing religious factions, and before Europeans had an inkling that the Americas and their indigenous inhabitants existed.

"In the beginning God created the heaven and the earth." Thus opens the Christian origin story, which, like the Wendat one, seeks to explain how hu-mans and animals and plants came into existence. This story had all the ele-ments to make it a favorite among Catholics, with, among other fantastic touches, a talking serpent and a whirling, flaming sword—not to mention powerful moral lessons. Among these lessons were some that resembled the teachings of the Wendat story: humans emerged from supernatural actions, the earth was plentifully supplied with animals and plants to sustain people, and human bones were connected with supernatural powers, as the Christian god created Eve out of Adam's rib.

But there were even more numerous points of divergence between the two stories. The Christian story described a world more clearly polarized between good and evil than the Wendat spiritual world with its shades of gray. In the Garden of Eden slithered a subtle serpent, representing the Devil and pure evil. God, by contrast, was wholly good, although paradoxically he allowed bad things to happen to rebuke those who did not obey him. Indeed, he punished Adam and Eve for eating the fruit of the tree of knowledge without his permission. God cursed Eve with the pain of childbirth: "in sorrow thou shalt bring forth children" (Gen. 3:16). For Adam God reserved the toil of farming. Outside the Garden of Eden, now guarded by the aforementioned sword to keep out the banished Adam and Eve, the fruit of the earth would not be nearly as abundant. Instead, God declared that man would earn bread only "in the sweat of thy face . . . till thou return unto the ground; for out of it wast thou taken; for dust thou art, and unto dust shalt thou return" (Gen. 3:19). Pain would forever be associated with the start of life, as well as with agriculture and the sustenance of life, until death returned all humans to dust. All humans thus inherited the stain of Adam's and Eve's "original sin."

This relatively bleak origin story did not distinguish Christianity from Judaism, as both religions shared the narrative of Adam and Eve. The difference was Jesus Christ. Christians believed that a mystical carpenter named Jesus from the town of Nazareth, not far from the Mediterranean Sea, was both god and man. He was the son of God, sent to earth to teach the "good news" that belief in him would lead to eternal life. His death upon the cross fulfilled Jesus's own teachings about the promise that became fundamental to Christianity: "For God so loved the world, that he gave his only begotten Son, that whosoever believeth in him should not perish, but have everlasting life" (John 3:16). For this reason the image of the dead or dying Jesus upon the cross became the central emblem of Catholicism. The Bible itself is restrained in its descriptions of the tortures received by Jesus: it mentions that he was scourged and beaten, and a crown of thorns placed on his head, and that he was crucified, but no gory details are given. By contrast, subsequent paintings and stained glass focused much more on what came to be called the "Passion" of Christ, the bodily tortures he endured. Fifteenth-century Catholics stood rapt before stained glass images of blood, glowing red when backlit by the sun, as it poured from their Savior.

Blood was also central to the holiest moment in the worship of fifteenth-century Catholics, the centerpiece of the Christian Mass: the sacrament of the Eucharist or Holy Communion. This ritual was based on Jesus's last supper with his disciples, when he broke bread and said, "Take, eat; this is my body," then raised a cup of wine and said, "Drink ye all of it; for this is my blood" (Matt. 26:26–28). Lay Catholics did not actually partake of the bread and wine that had been supernaturally transformed into the flesh and blood of Christ in the Mass; that was reserved for the priest. Nor did most French Catholics understand exactly what the priest was saying as he did so, for the language of the Mass was Latin. But it was a transcendent moment nonetheless to be in the actual presence of Jesus.

Christ's promise was eternal life, but this did not ensure a positive outcome for all Catholics. This was because Christians, unlike Wendats, believed that there were different destinations for the souls of humans depending on whether they were good or evil. The souls of the good went to heaven and those of the evil went to hell, but there was a third destination to which most souls were consigned, at least for a time: purgatory. The souls of those who were not entirely good or entirely evil went to purgatory, where they were purified by fire. Fortunate souls eventually saw an end to their purgation and God allowed them into heaven. In this they could be aided by the actions of the living: prayers for the souls of the dead and acts of charity on their behalf could speed their escape from purgatory. For this reason it has been said that the dead were omnipresent in Catholic Europe. The living were expected to be vigilant about the dead, frequently praying for their souls, so the dead were always on the minds of the living.

Fear that their own souls would wind up in purgatory or even hell was a powerful motivating force for fifteenth-century Catholics. Concerns about Satan led parents to seek protection for their children, and they found this security in the sacrament of baptism. This ritual cleansed infants of the inheritance of original sin. New parents could barely wait for baptism, sometimes dragging priests from their beds to perform it. When the parents and child reached the entrance to the church, the priest performed a potent rite of exorcism. This countered the power that the Devil had maintained over all newly born humans ever since the fall of humankind in the Garden of Eden. The priest addressed his remarks to the demon within the child: "I exorcise thee, unclean spirit, . . . accursed one, damned and to be damned." The parents then carried the newly purified child into the church, where the priest performed the actual baptism. He sprinkled the infant's head with holy water, "in the name of the Father, the Son, and the Holy Spirit." An infant who subsequently died before committing any sins was guaranteed a place in heaven, having been absolved by the power of the ritual. There was also a widespread folk belief (unsupported by official church doctrine) that, as one historian puts it, "baptism gave infants a better chance for survival, cured sick babies, and made handicapped ones whole."[1] Thus, both religious and medical concerns led parents to fervently seek baptism for their children.

For adults who needed protection from Satan or other malefactors, the most popular recourse was prayer to the saints. These individuals—the "very special dead"—were declared by the Pope to be saints in heaven who could intercede on behalf of the living.[2] It was not that the saints had special magical powers, but that because they dwelled beside Christ in heaven they could petition him to help the afflicted. Although the Pope was supposed to be the final arbiter on who had actually achieved the status of sainthood, ordinary Catholics did not always wait for the Vatican's imprimatur before praying to the soul of a local figure of extraordinary spiritual powers. As a result, there were literally thousands of "saints"—official and unofficial—to whom Catholics could pray for assistance. These prayers were especially effective if offered while handling or being close to relics—objects that the saint had touched during her life, or her bones. Sometimes the bodies of putative saints were even boiled so that people did not have to wait around until the body decomposed in order to divide the body into relics. This relic trade contributed to the omnipresence of the dead in Catholic Europe: every church contained saints' bones in elaborate reliquaries, special containers often made of gold and silver.

These, then, were the religious themes of greatest interest to lay Catholics circa 1450: the power of the crucified Christ to redeem them from sin and grant them eternal life, the presence of Christ in the ritual of the Eucharist, and the protection against the Devil provided by baptism and prayer to the saints. An issue that mattered little to ordinary Catholics, but that eventually had a profound impact on world history, was the relationship between Catholicism and the nation-state. In 1450 European nations were relatively weak, with only limited success in bringing a variety of city-states and provincial power centers under their control. This began to change in 1469 with the marriage of Isabella of Castile and Ferdinand of Aragon. The union of the provinces of Castile and Aragon laid the foundation for modern Spain, and modern nation-building in general.

Together, Isabella and Ferdinand were able to centralize power by reining in the nobility and gaining greater control over taxation. They also made Catholicism the centerpiece of their nation-building project. Spain had long been home to large numbers of Jews and Muslims, and it was these non-Christians that Ferdinand and Isabella sought to convert to Catholicism or purge from their new nation. The Spanish monarchs grandly hoped to use their dominion as a base for taking the holy city of Jerusalem from Muslim control and for spreading Catholicism to non-Christians everywhere. Ferdinand and Isabella gained a great victory in this battle against non-Catholics when in 1492 they conquered Granada, the last Muslim stronghold in Spain. Also in 1492, as part of their quest for religious "purity," they demanded that all Jews in the kingdom either convert to Catholicism or be expelled.

This context of militant Catholic optimism framed the Spanish monarchs' response to Christopher Columbus. In 1492 the Genoese navigator boldly requested that Ferdinand and Isabella finance his expedition to find a westward sea route to the valuable silks and spices of Asia. The rival Portuguese had pioneered this trade by sailing south and then east around Africa. Columbus had a better idea: sail west across the Atlantic and avoid the whole African detour. Ferdinand and Isabella agreed to finance Columbus's speculative journey because it closely aligned with their own economic and religious goals. If Columbus made it to Asia, he could expand their campaign of religious "purification" outside of Spain by converting untold millions to Christianity. And if the luxury goods he brought back were as valuable as expected, the profits would underwrite a crusade against the Muslims in Jerusalem.

Columbus, of course, did not make it to Asia. He did not count on North and South America lying between him and his goal. Columbus went to his death believing that he had reached "the Indies," islands near India and Japan (and thus he called the inhabitants *los indios*, or Indians). But other navigators soon realized that Columbus had discovered what was, from the European perspective, a "New World." This previously unknown territory could still fulfill the religious goals of the Spanish monarchs, by providing gold and silver—and converts to the holy Catholic faith.

But just as the fortunes of the Catholic Church seemed greater than ever, a threat emerged from within Europe: the Protestant Reformation. Traditionally said to have been initiated by the ninety-five theses or arguments Martin Luther nailed to the church doors in the German city of Wittenberg in 1517, the Reformation actually drew on a long tradition of Catholic reform. For centuries many Catholic leaders had sought to standardize the Church's ritual practices and to make its bureaucratic machinery more efficient. Luther, an Augustinian monk with an impressive knowledge of Church history and theology, was only the most recent of these reformers.

Although Luther initially conceived his ideas as a program to reform the Catholic Church from within, it soon became clear that his disagreements were too fundamental for the Church to accept. Thus, new faiths were formed outside the umbrella of the Catholic Church, dubbed "Protestant" denominations because they protested Catholic beliefs and Church hierarchy. This split within the dominant institution of Western Europe produced nearly a century of bloody religious warfare. These battles were especially ferocious in Germany and France, lands along the boundary between what eventually became, with some important exceptions, a predominantly Protestant northern Europe and a largely Catholic southern Europe.

Catholic leaders did not sit idly by as an ever-larger share of Europe's Christians embraced Protestantism. From 1545 to 1563 they crafted a response in a series of gatherings in the Italian alpine town of Trent. These meetings came to be known as the Council of Trent, and its decrees laid the foundation for the Catholic Reformation (sometimes called the Counter-Reformation): the attempt to reform and strengthen the Catholic Church in response to the Protestant challenge. Central to the Catholic Reformation were efforts to make sure that ordinary believers—from urban artisans to illiterate peasants—understood the tenets of the Church. Everywhere the byword was *education*, as Catholic leaders aimed to stamp out what they saw as superstitious and heterodox beliefs held by some lay Catholics. Clergymen traveled to places such as southern Italy and Brittany in the northwest corner of France to educate the masses in the finer points of Catholic theology.

This "domestic" or "internal" mission (internal to Europe, that is) complemented the "overseas" or "external" mission of bringing Catholicism to the New World and beyond. If Ferdinand and Isabella had been eager to spread Catholicism to the non-Christian parts of the world, that impulse became even stronger in the sixteenth century, as the rivalry with Protestantism spread to the Americas. Spain attempted to Christianize the indigenous people of the Caribbean islands, Mexico, and Peru. France likewise saw itself as carrying the Catholic standard overseas, but because of Spanish dominance in the south, France looked to the colder regions of North America such as Canada and northern New England. In 1541, for example, the king of France commissioned a voyage to North America with religious goals at the forefront. The king declared that the explorers should "inhabit the aforesaid lands and countries [of North America] and build there towns and fortresses, temples and churches, in order to impart our Holy Catholic Faith and Catholic Doctrine" to American Indians.[3]

In both overseas and domestic missions, Catholic clergymen attempted to spread a reinvigorated Catholic Reformation piety that emphasized prayer and internal spiritual discipline. There were many topics discussed by these clergymen, but among the most popular with lay European Catholics were issues revolving around healing and mortuary rituals—matters of life and death. Because these subjects also resonated powerfully with the American Indians whom the French missionaries encountered in the New World, it is worthwhile to examine French healing practices and deathways in the second half of the sixteenth century, as the impact of the Catholic Reformation began to be felt.

Healing was vitally important to French Catholics because they were surrounded by death and disease. By some measures, early modern France was less healthful than Wendake. Whereas the infant mortality rate in Wendake was roughly 120 to 180 per 1,000 live births, in France the rate ranged from 200 in rural areas to as high as 400 in poor urban neighborhoods. The latter figure means that 40 percent of children born in impoverished districts in Paris and other cities did not reach their first birthday. As a result, life expectancy at birth was lower in France (twenty-one years in cities and twenty-six years in the countryside) than in Wendake (thirty years). The cause of all this infant and childhood mortality in France was infectious disease. The French had to survive measles, influenza, smallpox, and occasional epidemics of bubonic plague in order to make it to adulthood. But once French people survived these diseases and became adults, they lived a bit longer than Wendats (to an average age of fifty-four compared to forty-nine), largely because of a food supply less prone to weather-induced shortages.

Surrounded by illness, the French interpreted healing as a combination of natural and supernatural elements. One important paradigm for understanding disease in early modern Europe was the theory of humors, which was based on the teachings of Galen of Pergamum, a second-century Greek physician. The human body, according to Galen, possessed four crucial humors or fluids: blood, phlegm, black bile, and yellow bile. Each humor had distinct qualities: blood was hot and wet, phlegm was cold and wet, black bile was cold and dry, and yellow bile was hot and dry. When a person's humors became imbalanced, she would suffer illness. According to humoral theory, the way to treat an imbalance was to apply its opposite. If a physician diagnosed a patient with too much cold and wet phlegm, he would prescribe products made out of plants or animals or minerals that were dry and hot to counter the phlegm. Medicinal cannibalism, or prescribing human tissue to cure disease, was fairly common. The accepted antidote for epilepsy, for example, included shavings of a human skull, preferably from a man who had met a violent death.

Working hand in glove with these natural remedies were supernatural cures. As the physician Ambroise Paré famously described the care he offered a patient, "I tended him, God cured him."[4] Indeed, Christianity had always been a healing religion; many of Christ's miracles involved healing the sick and even raising the dead. As a result, the first thing that most French Catholics did when they or their loved ones fell ill was to pray. Sometimes they prayed to Christ or the Virgin Mary, and sometimes to the saints, who were often associated with specific illnesses. St. Roch, for example, had suffered the plague and so victims of that scourge prayed to him. St. Erasmus had been killed by torturers who ripped out his entrails; he thus became the patron saint of stomach aches. Other connections were less direct: St. Cloud's name sounded like the French word for boils (*clous*), so those afflicted with abscesses and boils prayed to him.

But prayer by itself was not the only or even the most effective way to gain the intercession of a saint. More supernatural power could be gained by touching the holy person's bones while praying to that saint. Sometimes this required a pilgrimage: a journey of a day, a week, or perhaps even several months to reach the bones of an especially powerful saint. The hearing-impaired throughout France, for example, traveled to Paris to touch the finger of St. Ouen. More often, people availed themselves of the holy bones in the reliquaries of their own parish church.

During epidemics, these individual attempts to gain access to supernatural healing gave way to group efforts. Because epidemics struck so many people at once, they were interpreted as signs of God's anger at the sinfulness of the community. Clergymen warned their parishioners during epidemics that an angry God could be mollified only through communal rituals of repentance. When the worst epidemics—especially bubonic plague—struck France, lay Catholics needed little prompting to engage in these rituals. Sometimes an entire town would gather to vow improved behavior; other times they would attend a special Mass dedicated to asking God's forgiveness. But most popular was the ritual of the communal procession, in which the parish priest, carrying a cross or image of the Virgin Mary or a saint's relics, led an assemblage of solemn townspeople through the streets. In the town of Bourg-en-Bresse in the sixteenth century there were as many as fourteen of these processions *daily* during epidemics.

But, sadly for the zealous marchers of Bourg-en-Bresse and residents of countless other French towns, their efforts frequently could not halt the progress of infectious diseases. At some point in a person's illness, it often became clear that the person no longer occupied a sickbed but rather a deathbed. When this happened, the proceedings became semipublic, as friends and family members gathered to make sure that the person would not die alone. These witnesses were also interested in receiving the dying person's prayers and blessings. Although the French did not have a ritual as formalized as the Wendat farewell feast, they did place a great deal of weight on the words of a dying person, who was seen as straddling this world and the next. In fact, there was a tradition called the *Ars moriendi* or art of dying that specified proper deathbed behavior. The dying person was expected to dispense wisdom, forgive old grudges, and offer prayers for those gathered by the bedside.

As the person slipped ever closer to death, however, the stakes were raised because a supernatural battle with eternal consequences commenced. Catholics believed that as a person was dying there appeared around the deathbed angels and demons, representing good and evil. The dying person had the power to choose good or evil, as indicated by avoiding demonic deathbed temptations such as impatience or anger or questioning God's will. If, as prescribed by the *Ars moriendi* tradition, the dying person chose to side with angels, it did not mean that his soul was guaranteed to go to heaven, but it certainly helped.

It also helped to have the local priest perform the ritual of extreme unction or last anointing. When it seemed like the person was on the verge of death, a family member hurried to fetch the parish priest. The breathless priest quickly said prayers to try to ward off the wily demons. For further protection he offered the dying person the consecrated host—bread supernaturally transformed into the body of Christ. The priest then dipped his thumb in oil blessed by a bishop and anointed the dying person's eyelids, lips, and ear lobes—all places that may have committed or witnessed sins during the person's lifetime. The Council of Trent was unequivocal in its declaration that the anointing was not magical, but rather that it was "the grace of the holy Spirit, whose anointing takes away sins, if there are any still to be expiated."[5] Many lay Catholics likely did not make this fine of a distinction. What they did focus on was the importance of the entire deathbed scene, just as Wendats did.

French Catholics also resembled Wendats in the attention they paid to proper corpse preparation. This involved washing the body and wrapping it in a shroud made of linen or cerecloth, a waxed linen that helped contain the odors of decomposition. Offensive smells were an issue because the French generally waited a couple of days before burying the body. Between death and burial the body was never left alone; in an era when it was hard to tell exactly when a person died, this waiting period served to help prevent burial alive. Moreover, as the shrouded body lay in the family's home inside a coffin (which usually had been rented from the parish on account of the high cost of wood), it provided an opportunity to hold a wake. This gathering of friends and family was less sedate than the wakes most North Americans are accustomed to today. The wake was a time when community members wept and prayed, but they also drank and told off-color jokes about the deceased.

When the day of the funeral arrived, a procession formed to carry the coffined body from the home to the church. The procession made visible one of the important differences between France and Wendake: the greater status differentiation in European funerals, a mirror of Europe's more highly stratified society. Although Wendats did make distinctions between the funerals of highly respected individuals and those on the margins of society, they did not have nearly the vast differences between the funerals of French paupers and nobility. So when townspeople gathered for a funeral procession, there was a direct correlation between the deceased's social status and the number of people in the procession. Indeed, the wealthy often made provision in their wills to pay the poor to be in the procession, in what was seen as an act of charity.

But whether the deceased was rich or poor, the final destination of the procession was the church, where the body was laid in front of the altar and, if the deceased's will set aside some money for it, surrounded by candles. Here the priest performed the Requiem Mass, also known as the Funeral Mass, singing or chanting psalms and prayers. In the holiest moment of the proceedings, he raised the consecrated host, consuming the body of the crucified Savior. He then sprinkled the coffin with holy water and waved his thurible filled with burning incense over the body to signal the end of the Mass. In all, it was a feast for the senses: psalms resonated off soaring arches, the smell of beeswax and incense filled the air, and the warm glow of candlelight enveloped the worshippers.

The Mass over, it was time to bury the dead. The rich usually wanted to be buried within the church, which was very expensive owing to the limited space and the keen desire to be buried near the holy bones of saints held in reliquaries. For church burial the coffin might be slid behind a niche in the wall or laid under the stones beneath the very feet of the worshippers, furthering the extent to which the dead surrounded the living in Catholic France. Most people, however, had to settle for burial in the churchyard. Unable to afford even a coffin, most individuals were removed from their rented coffin and placed into an unmarked grave wearing only a shroud.

Because French churchyards were densely packed with the remains of the dead, gravediggers routinely encountered bones from previous burials. Unlike today, when most North Americans expect their burial plots to remain undisturbed in perpetuity, there was no such expectation in sixteenth-century France. Gravediggers opened the earth in places where no one had been buried in at least a few years, and when they inevitably found skulls and long bones and ribs, they carefully removed them, cleaned them, and placed them into the church's charnel house. Here they would remain, rich (or at least middling) and poor jumbled together, an apt symbol of the ties of community and humanity that united those divided by class status. Once safely ensconced in the charnel house, the bones attracted Catholics to come and pray for the souls of the deceased. Thus, just as in Wendake, secondary burial was commonplace in sixteenth-century France, even if in France it occurred anonymously, without awareness that a particular person was being disinterred and relocated.

But after the funeral a person's anonymous secondary burial was still years in the future. When the primary interment was completed, those in the funeral procession hungered for a feast. Here the logic approximated that in Wendake, even though it took place after the burial in France and before the burial in Wendake. In both places, the purpose of the event was to begin to repair the rent in the social fabric caused by the individual's death. In France, the deceased's will often provided money for abundant food and drink. Attendees drank wine and cider with abandon, which helped them focus on the positive: fond memories of the deceased and hopes that his or her soul was in heaven, or at least soon to be headed there.

After the feast, when the reality of the death sunk in, the bereaved sometimes went to pray in the cemetery. In stark contrast with Wendake, however, French cemeteries were not always treated with reverence. The French, to be sure, visited graveyards to pray and weep over the remains of the deceased, but they also used cemeteries—often the only open, centrally located space in a crowded French town—for a wide range of secular activities. People set up market stalls, played games, and allowed their pigs to root around in the loose soil (sometimes having to return a detached arm or leg to its rightful owner). Church leaders long tried to curb these practices, but to no avail. In 1617, for example, one official tried to ban not only "drying laundry, beating wheat, and holding fairs and markets" in cemeteries, but also "playing tennis or boules."[6] He argued that such activities turned what should be sacred ground into a playground. But he also said that dancing in the cemetery was fine, as long as it was part of a church marriage.

During the day French churchyards were the site of work and play, but at night they took on a more sinister aspect. Even though it was not part of orthodox Church teachings, ordinary Catholics believed that the souls of those in purgatory huddled in the cemeteries where they were buried. As in Wendake, the boundary between this world and the supernatural world was permeable indeed. These souls were generally benign and did not aim to trouble the living. They simply bided their time, in the popular imagination, until they were allowed to enter heaven. Some souls did haunt the living, however. If someone had failed to fulfill an obligation to the deceased, then the soul might return and try to remedy the problem. In French folktales it was common for a person's ghost to admonish his or her children not to forget to pray for their poor dead parent's soul. Improper burials also caused many hauntings. In sixteenth-century Brittany, a woman murdered her husband and hid the corpse in the family's salted-meat cellar. The ghost returned, told his brother what happened, and led the man to the body (carefully avoiding the hams and salt beef). On this evidence the woman was convicted and executed.

This was just the sort of folk belief that many clergymen, inspired by the Catholic Reformation, tried to stamp out or at least rein in. No group better epitomizes the teaching zeal of the Catholic Reformation than the Society of Jesus, whose members are known as Jesuits. This religious order was founded in 1540 by a Spanish nobleman named Ignatius of Loyola. Ignatius retired from military life, his primary pursuit, in 1521 after receiving a serious battlefield injury. During the 1520s the former soldier began to have increasingly intense spiritual cravings, experiencing visions of the Virgin Mary that convinced him to lay aside his former ways in favor of an ascetic religious life. Ignatius's charismatic personality and mystical experiences soon attracted other spiritual seekers. Ignatius and nine of these men became the first members of the Society of Jesus when the Pope incorporated the religious order in 1540.

From their founding the Jesuits bore the stamp of two distinct yet inter-twined aspects of Ignatius's personality and experience. First, his followers sought to imitate his intense and mystical relationship with Jesus Christ. In this they were guided by the *Spiritual Exercises*, a book written by Ignatius that outlined a focused period of prayer and contemplation that all Jesuits had to follow. The *Exercises* innovated by requiring potential recruits not to recite memorized prayers and set formulas, but to engage in focused contemplation and spontaneous prayer, always with the crucified Jesus in mind. As Ignatius urged, "Imagine Christ our Lord suspended on the cross before you, and con-verse with him in a colloquy."[7] This is how all potential Jesuits spent their first thirty days in the order: alone, silent, and in mental conversation with their bloody Savior.

Second, Ignatius drew on his military experience to emphasize order and organization. The Jesuits had a clear chain of command, which allowed them to mobilize money and zealous recruits for their spiritual warfare. For de-spite the intense inward focus on prayer, the Jesuits were no cloistered group of medieval monks. Instead, they were all about action, getting out into the world to teach and minister to the masses.

In particular, Ignatius responded to the challenge of Protestantism by de-claring spiritual warfare on the enemies of the Catholic Church. He and his followers educated the European poor through domestic missions and the Eu-ropean middling and upper classes in schools, seminaries, and colleges. They also turned their sights toward converting non-Christians outside of Europe. The first overseas mission the Jesuits undertook was in their very first year of existence: Francis Xavier sailed to India in 1540 to gain converts for Christ. When the French crown began to show interest in colonizing North America, the Jesuits weren't far behind. Many Jesuits expected or even hoped to die in their domestic or overseas missions; the allure of martyrdom was powerful. As one Jesuit wrote in a letter of 1570, "I hope that God . . . gives me the grace to die for the holy church and its doctrine."[8]

This emphasis on action and the potential for martyrdom attracted enor-mous numbers of dedicated young men who wanted to join the fight against ignorance and Protestantism (the two were not unrelated in their minds). The original ten members grew to a thousand by the time Ignatius died in 1556; by 1626 the Jesuits had 15,500 members. One of these bright young soldiers of Christ was Jean de Brébeuf, born in 1593 in Normandy in north-west France. From a landed family of lesser nobility, he had many options but chose the ascetic life of the Society of Jesus at the age of twenty-four.

Brébeuf entered the Jesuit novitiate or school for novices at Rouen in 1617, where he immediately embarked on the solitary thirty days of religious contemplation prescribed by the *Exercises*. During that time he meditated on the suffering and death of Jesus and perhaps longed for the glorious death of a martyr. He certainly did so later in his life; in a 1631 vow he combined the characteristically Catholic fascination with blood, death, and Christ's crucified body: "Lord Jesus, my Redeemer, you have ransomed me by your most precious blood and death. That is why I promise to serve you during my entire life in the Society of Jesus and to serve no one but you alone. I sign this promise in my blood and with my own hand and I am ready to sacrifice my whole life for you as gladly as this drop of blood."[9]

With a drop of his own blood Brébeuf sealed his willingness to give his life in the service of Christ. Only in Wendake—a place he could barely imagine in Rouen—would Brébeuf find out whether he would experience the glory of martyrdom.

three **First Encounters**

WE DON'T KNOW WHEN the Wendats first received a hint that for-eigners from an unknown land had arrived in North America. Nor do we know what that first hint was—perhaps an object made of hitherto unseen material, or a story of bearded men in strange costumes? We do know that by the 1570s, some forty years before Wendats encountered Frenchmen face-to-face, a few European goods had made their way into Wendake via long-established trad-ing routes with indigenous peoples who lived to the northeast.

Although it was probably not the very first European item in Wendake, an object that archaeologists call the "Sopher Celt" must have excited a great deal of curiosity among the Wendats. A celt (pronounced selt) is a tool shaped like a chisel or axe head, and "Sopher" is the archaeological site in Rock Nation territory where this one was found. This celt was heavy and pleasingly shaped, about the size of an axe head: four-and-a-half inches long, two inches wide, and weighing thirteen ounces.[1] If not the first European item in Wendake, it was among the earliest and most useful.

The first thing Wendats would have noticed about the Sopher Celt was the strange metal from which it was made: iron. American Indians did not have ironworking technology before European contact, so all of their knives and blades were made of stone or bone. Iron was a European commodity so unusual and desirable that when the French arrived in Wendake, the Wendats dubbed them *Agnonha*, "iron people."[2]

The second thing they would have admired in the Sopher Celt was the sharpness of its blade. Some native edged tools, to be sure, could be razor sharp, especially those made out of rare obsidian. But the Sopher Celt and items like it held their edges longer than most stone tools and were more easily sharpened when they became dull. Iron axes could cut down trees two to four times faster than their stone counterparts.

But perhaps the most revealing detail about the Sopher Celt is that, despite its utility and rarity, Wendats placed it inside a bundle burial at the bottom of a Feast of the Dead ossuary. Indeed, it would be more correct to say that the celt was buried *because* of its uniqueness and desirability. For Wendats, trade with Europeans brought many useful items to Wendake, not just celts and axes but fishhooks, awls, and copper kettles. All of these items were coveted because they helped make life a little easier for Wendats as they went fishing or prepared *sagamité*. But Wendats also interpreted these objects within a cultural framework in which goods were acquired in large part so they could be buried with the dead or given away at funerals. This serves as an apt analogy for the broader dynamic of Wendat-French encounters. Wendats interpreted almost every aspect of French religion and material culture with this question in mind: how will it affect our relationship with the dead?

In the decade or two after the Sopher Celt's arrival in Wendake, Wendats increased their trade with Algonquian Indians who lived to the northeast, in part to get more of the powerful and mysterious goods made of copper and iron that they brought with them. One winter, as was customary, a group of these Algonquians visited Rock Nation territory as part of their yearly travels to trade furs—and now iron tools—for dried Wendat corn. The Algonquian headman asked the Wendats if they would like to join him on a raid against the hated Iroquois, aided by the strangers who supplied iron hatchets and copper kettles. A Wendat warrior named Ochasteguin jumped at the opportunity, perhaps hoping to meet these metalworking outsiders. When spring arrived, he marshaled about twenty other warriors and asked the Algonquians to lead them to the strangers' settlement. The year was 1609.

Awaiting the arrival of his native allies was Samuel de Champlain, the French cartographer and navigator who just one year earlier had founded the first permanent French settlement in North America: Quebec. The French had long fished and traded along the northeast coast of North America, but a permanent inland settlement gave them a base from which to expand their mercantile—and soon, it was hoped, their spiritual—interactions with the natives.

As the Wendats and Algonquians swiftly paddled downstream on what the French called the St. Lawrence River, they reached a small island some fifty miles shy of their destination of Quebec. There, on about June 18, 1609, Wendats first encountered Europeans. Champlain, getting impatient, had left Quebec a few days earlier, but now he was delighted to see the large assembly of warriors, "men skilled in war and full of courage," as Ochasteguin proudly put it. At the request of the Indians, Champlain and his men fired their arquebuses, heavy muskets that were fired with a lighted fuse. The powder flashed and roared; Wendats, who had never before seen a gun, responded with "loud shouts of astonishment."[3] Two days of feasting followed, to celebrate the new alliance between the Wendats and the French.

Eventually the merriment of this first encounter gave way to the serious business at hand: continuing the expedition to attack the Mohawks, the easternmost of the Five Nations of Iroquois. For several decades the Mohawks had been sending war parties north to gain control of the St. Lawrence River Valley. They did so in order to get better access to European goods and to take advantage of the valley's rich hunting and fishing grounds. Soon they would have an alternate route to trade with Europeans: the Dutch arrived on the Hudson River just east of Mohawk territory later in 1609. In coming decades this allowed the Mohawks to cease their raids on the St. Lawrence, but for now they were still eager to hold on to the strategic valley. Later, after the Dutch founded the settlement of Fort Orange (later Albany) in 1624, the Mohawks traded furs with the Dutch for iron tools and eventually guns. When the Mohawks gained a steady supply of firearms, it changed the balance of power throughout the region, much to the detriment of the Wendats, but that was still several decades in the future.

In 1609 the Mohawks did not possess firearms, so they were at a disadvantage when they met the Wendats, Algonquians, and French on July 29. Wendats told Champlain that he would recognize the three Mohawk headmen by the great size of their feather headdresses. As the two sides advanced on one another, Champlain spotted the gaudily decorated enemy leaders. He loaded his arquebus with four lead balls and fired. The noise that had so astonished the Wendats had an even greater effect on the Mohawks, because Champlain's roaring weapon killed two of the Mohawk leaders instantly, even though they held shields of cotton and wood that effectively repelled arrows. Taking advantage of the Mohawks' surprise, the Wendats and Algonquians rushed forward and "began to shout so loudly that one could not have heard it thunder."[4] Energized by these war whoops, Champlain's allies routed the Mohawks. The French-Wendat alliance was off to an auspicious start.

The Rock Nation warriors returned to Wendake with stories about their glorious victory and their new French allies. They decided that every spring they would make the nine-hundred-mile journey by canoe to Quebec in order to trade with the French. They made this arduous trip six times before the French reciprocated and visited Wendake in 1615. Champlain, cartography pens in his hands and gunmen by his sides, reached Wendake in August. He was immediately impressed by the "enormous" fish in the lakes and the "very pleasant" landscape. He was also interested in Wendat healing practices and mortuary rituals, providing the first European description of the Feast of the Dead. He was curious enough about this impressive event that he correctly discerned its social importance: "just as their bones are collected and united in one and the same place, so also during their lives they should be united in friendship and harmony as relatives and friends, without the possibility of separation."[5]

The other French visitor that summer was of a different sort than Champlain and his soldiers. Joseph Le Caron was a Catholic missionary, not a Jesuit but a Récollet. This religious order (a reformist branch of the Franciscans) got its name from its members' fondness for meditation or recollection. Like the Jesuits, they combined their inward meditations with an outwardly directed missionary spirit. Unlike the Jesuits, the Récollets were a mendicant order, relying on alms for funding, and thus poorer than their rivals. Le Caron spent the winter of 1615–1616 in Wendake, more on a scouting expedition than a full-fledged effort to gain converts. He learned a bit of the language and worked on a dictionary that would be of great use to his successors. In 1616 Le Caron returned to Quebec.

Owing to a shortage of funds, French missionaries did not return to Wendake until 1623. During the seven years between missionary visits, life in Wendake returned to the routine of farming, fishing, and annual trade convoys to

Quebec. When Le Caron returned in 1623, he was accompanied by two other Récollets, Nicolas Viel and Gabriel Sagard. The latter, a young man with an observant eye, published an account of his experiences called *The Long Journey to the Country of the Hurons* (1632). It is his perspective on the Récollet interactions with the Wendats that survives; the Wendat view is lost.

Like Champlain, Sagard was impressed by the Wendats and their surroundings. Wendake was, in Sagard's opinion, "full of fine hills, open fields," and "very beautiful broad meadows." Wendats garnered even more praise. Sagard described them as the "aristocracy" of Canadian Indians because of their sedentary way of life, which more closely resembled French ideas of "civilization" than the nomadic lifestyle of hunter-gatherers to the north. The Wendats' only beverage was water, which meant that they were able to avoid the quarreling and debauchery that was so common among drunkards in France. Their healthy diet and lack of alcohol gave them splendid physiques and "marvelously white" teeth. They were especially well built in comparison with French men: among the Wendats "there are none indeed of those big-bellied men, full of humours [i.e., fluids] and fat, that we have" in France.[6]

To be sure, Sagard found some Wendat customs distasteful. He was disgusted by mothers who cleaned their children by picking off and eating lice. And, as a young man who had made a vow of perpetual chastity, he was especially troubled by the Wendats' carefree attitude toward adolescent sexuality. But on balance he found many more things to admire about the Wendats, such as their hospitality toward guests (from which he benefited greatly in 1623), their gravity and thoughtfulness in conversation, and their generosity toward needy members of their community.

One other aspect of Wendat society received special praise: their deathways. Again and again, Sagard contrasted the Wendats' assiduous care for the dying and dead with the relative indifference of the French. In this Sagard undoubtedly was advancing a polemic; he hoped to inspire his French readers to increase their devotions to the dead. But because Sagard's descriptions are in line with all other accounts of Wendat deathways, it does not seem that he exaggerated. For example, Sagard liked to visit the village cemetery so he could watch Wendats attend to their dead. While observing the bereaved, he "admired the care that these poor people take of the dead bodies of their deceased relatives and friends." Indeed, he felt that "in this respect they surpass the piety of Christians, since they spare nothing for the relief of the souls [of the departed], which they believe to be immortal and in need of help from the living."[7] Sagard admired the gravity and order of the Wendat cemeteries, in stark contrast to the rooting pigs and marriage dances of French graveyards.

And like Champlain and every other French observer of the Wendats, Sagard was impressed by the Feast of the Dead. After describing one of these elaborate ceremonies, he addressed his French readers directly: "Christians, let us reflect a little and see if our zeal for the souls of our relations, detained in God's prisons [purgatory], is as great as that of the poor savages for the souls of their dead in like circumstances, and we shall find that their zeal is more intense than ours, and that they have more love for one another, both in life and after death, than we who call ourselves better."[8]

Because of the Wendat belief in immortality and their admirable attention to the dead, Sagard thought it would be relatively easy to convert them to Catholicism. But, less than a year after they arrived, he and Le Caron were forced to leave Wendake as a result of the Récollet shortage of funds. Wendats seem to have observed these early comings and goings of French missionaries with something of a jaded eye. Wendats listened politely to the priests, that much is true. But this reflected one of the central rules of Wendat etiquette: listen carefully when someone is speaking, and if you disagree, keep quiet rather than offer intemperate counterarguments.

Still, many Wendats seem to have been curious about the French holy men and their proclaimed mastery of the supernatural. Perhaps they hoped the priests would be able to provide an additional means of communication with the all-important world of the dead. Two years later French officials asked the Wendats to host three priests, including Jean de Brébeuf, and it took only a few extra presents to convince them to allow the holy men to join the annual convoy of canoes from Quebec to Wendake. The Wendats would have noticed one immediate difference between these men and those who preceded them: whereas Sagard and his Récollet companions wore the undyed sheep's wool habit that in Europe earned their order the nickname of Greyfriars, Brébeuf and the other newcomers were outfitted in the distinctive Jesuit vestment that led Wendats to refer to them, somewhat derisively, as Black Robes.

Another difference between the Récollets and Jesuits was not visible to the naked eye. The Jesuit philosophy of conversion, initiated by Francis Xavier and elaborated in the second half of the sixteenth century, showed greater tolerance toward "matters of indifference," local customs that did not directly contradict the teachings of the Catholic Church. Alessandro Valignano, an Italian Jesuit missionary to Asia, called this *il modo soave*, the "gentle way" to conversion. As Valignano put it in his 1579 instructions to Jesuit missionaries in China and Japan, "Do not attempt in any way to persuade these people to change their customs, their habits, and their behavior, as long as they are not evidently contrary to religion and morality."[9]

The gentleness of the "gentle way" should not be exaggerated; Jesuits were steadfast in their opposition to customs that directly contradicted Catholic teachings, such as plural marriage. But they were willing to overlook customs that seemed to have no religious significance, including some feasts and dances. In practice, this led the Jesuits to depart from the Récollets in their conversion tactics. The Récollets thought they would have the greatest success by finding Wendat boys they could send to Quebec or even France for religious instruction, so as to insulate them from the "uncivilized" practices of their friends and family members. The Jesuits, by contrast, mostly sought to work within Wendat villages, where they hoped their converts would serve as role models for others.

In this the Jesuits also differed from other missionaries in North America, in particular the Puritans who would later try to convert New England's Algonquian Indians to Protestantism. New England's most famous missionary, John Eliot, started from the assumption that natives would have to be sequestered in "praying towns," where they would adopt English culture before they could imbibe Protestant religion. Starting in 1650, with the founding of the praying town of Natick, Massachusetts, Eliot tried to force Indians interested in Christianity into adopting English hairstyles, clothing, dwellings, and agricultural practices. Only then, he believed, would they be ready to learn about Jesus Christ.

The Jesuits employed a very different approach. They did not want to isolate Wendats in praying towns—thus Brébeuf's nine-hundred-mile journey to Wendake in 1626. Brébeuf and his companions felt that Wendat villages were the best places to try to gain converts. And Brébeuf did not try to get Wendats to cut their hair in the French style or to wear European clothing. He may have assumed that Wendats would eventually do so as they became more "civilized," but this was not a necessary first step toward conversion.

Such questions about missionary methods would have seemed distant and abstract, however, as Brébeuf shakily climbed into a rocking canoe in the summer of 1626. Of much more immediate concern was whether Brébeuf was going to survive the journey to Wendake. Not only was the missionary unable to swim, but his great height (his friends punned on the pronunciation of his last name by calling him a *vrai boeuf*, a "real ox") made it seem like the birchbark canoe was always about to tip over.[10] His size and strength would have been assets had he been required to paddle, but his hosts generously allowed him to avoid that difficult task. For nearly a month Brébeuf squeezed himself into the canoe and traveled in near silence as his Wendat guides labored against the current.

Freedom from paddling notwithstanding, Brébeuf did endure other deprivations alongside the Wendats, whose customs he had to accommodate himself to. Provisions were meager for everyone, usually just a few handfuls of dried corn and water, especially when the Wendats couldn't find the food caches they had hidden on the trip to Quebec. The rivers included many rocky rapids and waterfalls that required the men to get out and drag the canoes and carry their supplies. Mosquitoes and black flies tormented them at night when all they wanted to do was sleep. And Brébeuf could only barely communicate with his hosts. He had been chosen for this mission because of his extraordinary facility with languages, already demonstrated among the Montagnais Indians who lived near Quebec. But at this point his knowledge of Wendat was rudimentary.

This was one of the reasons Brébeuf would make little headway toward his goal of converting Wendats to Christianity—in addition to the fact that the Wendats felt no pressing need to embrace a new religion. When the Wendats and their French guests finally made it to Wendake after a strenuous month of paddling, Brébeuf and two other Jesuits took up residence in the village of Toanché. This was the first village the convoy came to, in the territory of the Bear People in the far northwestern corner of Wendake. In characteristically hospitable fashion, the residents of Toanché asked the Jesuits to reside in their longhouses with them. Brébeuf and his companions demurred, preferring instead the seclusion of a cabin built on the outskirts of the village. The Wendats were probably taken aback by this rejection of hospitality, but they likely kept their thoughts to themselves, in line with Wendat standards of politesse.

Few records survive of Brébeuf's time in Toanché, so we do not know what his daily routine was. But it likely included a great deal of language study. Brébeuf knew that he would have to learn the Wendat language if he had any hope of teaching his hosts about Catholicism. He was armed with word lists compiled by Le Caron and Sagard, but most of his learning took place orally, by attempting conversations with Wendats and repeatedly asking them to ex-

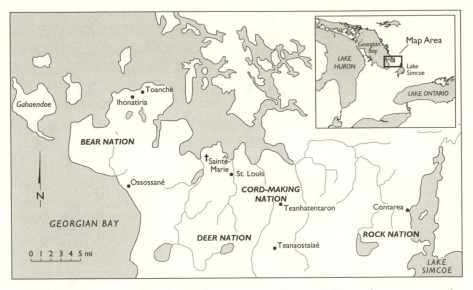

Wendake. Drawn by Bill Nelson, after maps in Trigger, *Children of Aataentsic*, and Warrick, *Population History of the Huron-Petun*.

plain words and phrases. The natives occasionally used their power over lin-guistically ignorant newcomers to make fun of them. As one Jesuit reported from a different locale, the Indians "sometimes palmed off on us indecent words, which we went about innocently preaching for beautiful sentences from the Gospels." Brébeuf himself complained about the "mockery" heaped upon those who struggled with the Wendat language.[11]

An even more serious problem for the Jesuits was the lack of Wendat words needed to convey the tenets of Christianity. The Wendat language, of course, lacked words for names unique to Christianity such as "Jesus," but these were easily enough supplied with Wendat neologisms (*Iesus*). For the Christian god the Jesuits eventually settled on the Wendat phrase that meant "Great Voice," as when describing the tortures of hell: "the Great Voice will punish your body."[12] But there were countless biblical terms for which there was no counterpart in Wendat: mundane words with allegorical implications such as sheep, shepherd, wine, and olives; words denoting the hierarchical relations of an alien society, such as master, lord, and servant; and religious concepts central to Christianity such as Trinity and Holy Spirit. Linguistic barriers thus made the work of Brébeuf and his fellow Jesuits extremely difficult for several years.

If we know little about Brébeuf's years in Toanché, we know even less about how Wendats viewed him. From other sources we know that Wendats found certain French customs puzzling or downright strange. Wendat men, who had sparse facial hair and yanked out what little there was with shell tweezers, found French beards disgusting. They thought that the black robes after which the Jesuits were mockingly named were both effeminate and highly impractical for getting around either by canoe or by foot. And, in light of the Wendat belief that unmarried adolescents were free to explore their sexuality with multiple partners, they found Jesuit celibacy curious and even slightly ominous. What kind of supernatural powers did Brébeuf and the others wield?

An incident from the end of Brébeuf's second year in Toanché suggests how the Wendats may have answered that question. The summer of 1628 was marked by a terrible drought in Wendake. The region's sandy soils made drought an ever-present threat, because without steady rains the earth quickly became parched. But this year Toanché seemed to be even drier than nearby villages. Many times that summer the residents of Toanché watched as storm clouds gathered in the distance and brought precious rains to nearby villages, but then at the last moment they dissipated and left Toanché as dry as before. Tehorenhaegnon, a powerful shaman, leveled an explosive accusation: the thunderbird that brought the rain was afraid of the red painted cross that stood proudly before the Jesuits' cabin. The village elders approached Brébeuf. "My nephew," they said, using a kinship term to signal their ties with the French, "we are of the opinion that you should take down that cross, and hide it awhile in your cabin, or even in the lake, so that the thunder and the clouds may not see it, and no longer fear it; and then after the harvest you may set it up again."

Brébeuf first responded with logic: the red cross had stood in front of his cabin for over a year, and it had rained many times in that period. When that didn't convince the elders, he made a bold gambit. "Since Tehorenhaegnon says that the thunder is afraid of this color of the cross, if you like we will paint it another color, white, or black, or any other; and if, immediately after, it begins to rain, you will be sure Tehorenhaegnon has told the truth; but if not, that he is an impostor." The elders took Brébeuf up on his offer. They painted the cross white but nothing happened; several days passed and no rain fell. The elders agreed that Tehorenhaegnon had been proven wrong: the thunderbird was not afraid of the red cross. Brébeuf did not stop there.

Taking advantage of the attention the incident had generated, he repainted the cross red, added a wooden representation of the bloody Christ, and taught the Wendats how to kiss the cross and offer prayers to it. They did so and, lo and behold, it began to rain.[13]

This incident reveals not only that Brébeuf was very lucky (what would he have said if it started pouring just as they were painting the cross white?), but also that he was operating very much on Wendat terms. The showdown with the shaman did little to teach the Wendats about Christianity. Some villagers learned that kissing the cross could make it rain, but they likely interpreted the cross as a charm, like the ones they sometimes found in the forest or fashioned out of bone or wood. The main lesson they drew was that Brébeuf was a shaman to be reckoned with, perhaps even more powerful than Tehorenhaegnon. Here was a new shaman who might be able to alter their relationship with the spirit world, for good or ill.

Brébeuf did not have much time to build on the dramatic victory over his magical rival. In 1629 he and his fellow Jesuits received word that they had to hurry back to Quebec. The English had defeated the French in a battle to control the St. Lawrence River and were taking control of the colony. England and France had brought their rivalry from Europe to North America, with the English trying to elbow their way into French territory as a way to gain access to the valuable northern fur trade. When the French were defeated, they could no longer guarantee the safety of the Jesuits, as Protestants now controlled Quebec. French officials therefore demanded that the priests return from their mission. Brébeuf left Toanché having baptized only one Wendat, an infant boy on the verge of death. Dejected, Brébeuf and the other Jesuits canoed to Quebec and then sailed for France.

Back in Europe Brébeuf itched to resume his missionary work. He did not have to wait long to return to Canada. France regained control of Quebec in 1632, and the following year Brébeuf and three other Jesuits made their way to the colony. Brébeuf, at age thirty-nine, was no longer a young man, but with a strong constitution and the fervor of one who is convinced of the righteousness of his cause, he was more than ready to face the difficulties of backcountry travel and long Canadian winters. In 1634 he joined the annual trading convoy back to Wendake.

This time Brébeuf had to help paddle his canoe. It must have seemed only fair to the Wendats that this ox of a man would pitch in and help the group reach its destination in a timely fashion. Brébeuf tried to keep his mind off the monotonous toil of paddling by counting the number of times they had to portage around rapids: thirty-five times they got out and carried their baggage, fifty times they dragged the canoes. Once again poor food, biting insects, and stony sleeping areas made stopping only marginally more comfortable than paddling.

On August 5 the convoy reached the shores of Wendake. Brébeuf fell to his knees and thanked his god that he had arrived safely, but his initial joy soon turned to concern. Where Toanché once stood there remained only ruins of longhouses. He realized that the village must have moved, as all Wendat villages did every ten or twelve years when corn cultivation exhausted the surrounding soils. Brébeuf dragged his baggage about two miles until he found the new village, now named Ihonatiria, with ten longhouses and about three hundred residents within the palisade.

The villagers greeted Brébeuf warmly, calling him by the Wendat name they had previously given him: Echon (eh-shon), an attempt to pronounce his given name of Jean. Brébeuf responded in kind, although his Wendat remained rusty for some time. When he tried to translate the phrase "guardian angel," for example, he unwittingly used the ungrammatical Wendat construction *aesken de iskiacarratas*, literally "I am the dead, who, you take care of me." The Wendats must have been both amused by and leery of this supernatural visitor who confidently intoned, "I am the dead!"[14]

Generous hosts that they were, the villagers immediately lodged Brébeuf alongside several Wendat families in the most comfortable longhouse in Ihonatiria. They then set about building the Jesuits what might be called a shorthouse: a truncated version of the traditional Wendat dwelling, commonly used for guests. It was twenty feet wide and twenty feet high, like a regular longhouse, but only thirty feet long. Still, it was a very generous gesture on the part of the Ihonatiria residents to spend six weeks building the structure. After they moved in, Brébeuf, his two Jesuit companions, and their three hired French servants divided the house into three rooms: an anteroom that doubled as a storage area for dried corn, a central area where they slept on reed mattresses and covered themselves with furs, and a back room that served as a chapel where they could pray and celebrate Mass daily. Only the chapel, with its crucifix and prayer books, indicated that this was not a Wendat guest house.

Brébeuf took up where he left off five years earlier, trying to find Wendat listeners for his discourses about Catholicism and using deathways to make an impression on his audience. In this regard there was one great difference between Ihonatiria and Toanché that greatly aided his cause. Whereas Toanché had been healthy during his three years there, Ihonatiria was struck with epidemic disease as soon as the French arrived. Indeed, sickness was first evident on the canoe voyage from Quebec to Wendake, and by autumn the residents of Ihonatiria reeled from an onslaught of disease unlike any they had ever witnessed.

It may seem unlikely that Wendats had not yet experienced epidemics of European diseases, given that they had been trading directly with the French for twenty-five years. Our image of early encounters between Europeans and Indians is that as soon as the bearded newcomers set foot in the New World, the microbes they unknowingly carried unleashed "virgin soil" epidemics, so called because the indigenous population had not been previously exposed to the viruses and therefore did not have any immunity to them. This made the population fertile ground for the spread of disease.

There is no doubt that virgin soil epidemics took a horrible toll on indigenous people throughout the Americas. Devastation caused by European diseases helped smooth the way for European colonization from Tierra del Fuego to Hudson Bay. But these epidemics did not always occur immediately after first contact with Europeans. Most infectious diseases have a communicable period of less than two weeks. The ocean voyage in the sixteenth and early seventeenth centuries took from four to six weeks; the crossing therefore served as a quarantine for those who may have begun the voyage with influenza or other sicknesses. By the time they arrived in the New World, most were no longer contagious. Perhaps even more importantly, the majority of infectious diseases in Europe—including measles and smallpox—occurred in children, who then acquired a lifelong immunity. Because children almost never made the transatlantic crossing in the sixteenth century, this potential vector of transmission was nearly eliminated. The Wendats, therefore, had never before (it seems) suffered an epidemic of European disease.

In 1634, however, children arrived in Quebec for the first time. Ten French families with about twenty-five children disembarked in June of that year, hoping to find economic opportunities in the fledgling colony. The children evidently brought measles with them from France. Wendats trading at Quebec that summer soon showed signs of sickness. On the voyage back to Wendake many became ill. By the autumn of that year, a full-blown epidemic raged in Ihonatiria. The symptoms, according to Brébeuf, were severe: "This sickness began with violent fever, which was followed by a sort of measles or smallpox, different, however, from that common in France, accompanied in several cases by blindness for some days, or by dimness of sight, and terminated at length by diarrhea which has carried off many and is still bringing some to the grave."[15] The disease struck at the worst time of the year, right in the middle of harvest when all hands were needed to bring in the bountiful corn crop. Instead, people lay in their longhouses, weak and feverish and frightened by this unfamiliar malady. Before it ended that winter, the epidemic killed perhaps 20 percent of Ihonatiria's residents, some 60 out of 300. Every longhouse was touched by death—except the Jesuit residence, that is. The Black Robes remained curiously, even supernaturally, healthy.

Brébeuf was impressed during the epidemic by Wendat courage in the face of death. He admired their "patience in their poverty, famine, and sickness." According to Brébeuf, Wendats approached death with a fearlessness that was the envy of Christians. "They receive indeed the news of death," he wrote, "with more constancy than those Christian gentlemen and ladies to whom one would not dare to mention it. They hear of it not only without despair, but without troubling themselves, without the slightest pallor or change of countenance."[16] Christians were supposed to be unperturbed as they were dying, knowing that it was God's will and hoping that their soul was bound for heaven. Wendats, Brébeuf argued, showed the kind of courage that most Christians could only hope for. In Brébeuf's optimistic interpretation, this Wendat character trait made them prime candidates for conversion to Christianity.

Brébeuf therefore seized upon the opportunity afforded by the epidemic to try to interest the stoic residents of Ihonatiria in Catholic deathways. His first step was to adopt the role of a healer, a figure common in both France and Wendake, and he used natural and supernatural methods to help the sick. In the former category, he offered remedies commonly used in France: precious raisins and prunes, and soup made from freshly caught game. The dried fruits were so popular that people came from nearby villages to get their hands on some. The supernatural remedy he offered consisted chiefly of prayer. As he went from longhouse to longhouse, he prayed with the sick. Some Wendats welcomed these magical incantations, whereas others likely wondered what he was muttering about.

Wendat opinions were even more sharply divided about another supernatural practice—baptism—that Brébeuf performed when the sick were on the verge of death. Some Catholic missionaries in the Americas, especially

Franciscans in New Spain, were willing to baptize hundreds of Indians at a time "by aspersion," a mass ritual of sprinkling holy water. Jesuits criticized this method for leaving the natives ignorant of the basic tenets of Christianity. Instead, Jesuits resolved to baptize only those who learned about Catholic doctrine and who adopted Christian behavioral norms such as monogamous marriage.

The dying were the one exception to this rule. Because the fate of a soul hung in the balance, Jesuits were willing to baptize the dying just before death, believing that if they did so the person's soul would go to heaven, as the person did not have an opportunity to sin after the cleansing ritual. This was a moment of great happiness for the Jesuits, who had come thousands of miles to, as they believed, save Wendat souls. As one Jesuit put it, "The joy that one feels when he has baptized an Indian who dies soon afterwards, and flies directly to Heaven to become an Angel, certainly is a joy that surpasses anything that can be imagined."[17]

Only once during Brébeuf's first tour of duty in Wendake in the late 1620s did he baptize a Wendat, an infant boy who was all but dead. When Echon returned in 1634, he was delighted to find that the boy had recovered from his illness and was now a "gentle" and healthy five-year-old. Unsurprisingly, this boy's family was impressed by the power of baptism, and so they were among those most eager to be "struck with water," as the Jesuits called the ritual in the Wendat tongue.[18] The first four people that Brébeuf baptized in Ihonatiria lived in the same longhouse as the miraculously restored boy.

Although Brébeuf did not describe the performance of the ritual, it almost certainly included Latin prayers for the dying person's soul, brief instructions in Wendat about Christ's redeeming blood, and the climactic anointing of the sick person's forehead with holy water. While tracing the pattern of the cross on the person's forehead with his moistened fingers, the priest intoned that the dying person was baptized "Nomine Patris, Filii, et Spiritus Sancti." We can imagine the power and mystery of this ritual, with its use of water and invocation of blood, its incomprehensible incantations, and the solemn tone and gestures of the Black Robe. For this reason a small number of Ihonatiria residents were eager to receive baptism, thinking that it would help them recover from the disease. Of the hundreds who were sick that autumn, Brébeuf baptized nine, at least two of whom survived.

But power and mystery could also stoke fear. In his descriptions of the epidemic, Brébeuf focused on those who asked to be baptized. He left unstated the fact that only nine Wendats wanted to be baptized, even though sixty died and many more than that were made deathly ill by a mysterious malady. The large majority probably wondered why the ritual was performed only on those who were about to die. Did it cause them to die? Why did almost no one recover after being struck by water? And why, if this was supposed to be a healing ritual, did the Black Robes talk so much about the spirit world while performing the ritual?

Because of this split of opinion among the Wendats, deathbed scenes became highly contested in Ihonatiria that autumn. When he visited some dying Wendats, Brébeuf was rebuffed in his efforts to baptize or even instruct them. When he visited others, he learned of supernatural events that demonstrated how difficult the transition to Christianity would be for most Wendats. For both the Wendats and the French, deathbeds were charged moments, as the dying person lingered between this world and the next. In both cultures, the dying person was more open to communication with the spirit world than at any other time. Thus, Brébeuf took it very seriously when dying Wendats reported supernatural visitations.

This happened with a man named Joutaya, who suffered from disease along with so many of his fellow villagers. Joutaya was the father of the miraculously recovered boy, so he was among those most interested in being struck by water while he was dying. He was also willing to receive instruction about Christianity, which Brébeuf gladly provided. But then Joutaya reported a troubling supernatural visitation. As Brébeuf put it, "the Devil appeared to him in the form of one of his deceased brothers." This is almost certainly a revision of the man's words. It is much more likely that Joutaya simply stated that he had been visited by his dead brother's spirit; dying Wendats frequently reported similar supernatural interventions. Brébeuf probably insisted to Joutaya that this was the Devil masquerading as his brother, and this is how Brébeuf recorded the incident. Significantly, however, Echon did not dismiss the man's claim of communication with the spirit world.

The brother/Devil entered Joutaya's longhouse without greeting the dying man—a clear breach of Wendat social protocol. He then sat on the side of the fire opposite the dying man for a long time without saying anything. Joutaya must have wondered why his brother's spirit was angry with him. Eventually he found out. The spirit asked Joutaya, "How now, my brother, do you wish to leave us?" This was a clear reference to Joutaya's flirtation with Christianity. By accepting baptism, he threatened to "leave" the religious world of his ancestors. Unnerved, Joutaya tried to win back the favor of the spirit world. "No, my brother," he replied, "I don't wish to leave you; I will not leave you." The spirit was mollified. He moved closer to the dying man and tenderly caressed him.

This must have brought Joutaya momentary comfort, but it did not resolve his dilemma about whether to accept the healing magic of the Black Robes. When Joutaya told Brébeuf about the incident, Brébeuf's disappointment must have been obvious, because the dying man then insisted that he was not renouncing his baptism. According to Brébeuf, Joutaya "declared several times that he desired to go to Heaven."[19] For Wendats such as Joutaya, the appeal of Christianity was tempered by the knowledge that accepting baptism marked a break with the beliefs of their ancestors.

This ambivalence was less marked for those who seemed to be cured by the Black Robes' magical practices. These were the Wendats who served as living advertisements of the power of baptism. One such individual was a woman named Oquiaendis, the mother of the village headman and thus a respected and well-connected elder. She too lived in the longhouse of the boy who appeared to have been cured by baptism in Toanché. When she sickened that autumn, she asked Brébeuf to baptize her. All her strength was gone and she appeared on the very brink of death, yet, according to Brébeuf, "as soon as she was washed with the sacred waters she began to improve." Before long she was entirely well. Even more heartening, from Brébeuf's perspective, was that Oquiaendis went around telling everyone she saw that they should be struck with water. Given her age and social status, many must have listened carefully to her words.

Others who received baptism were not so fortunate, but even in death they could advance Brébeuf's strategy of using deathways to impress the Wendats. Tsindacaiendoua was an old man of roughly eighty years, "one of the best-natured" Wendats Brébeuf had ever met. As he lay dying, he asked for the healing waters of baptism. The ritual did not cure him; he was too far gone. But as the man approached his end, he must have asked Brébeuf to bury him outside the village cemetery, for in light of the issue's sensitivity Brébeuf would not have done so without his permission. So instead of being placed into a bark coffin on a scaffold near the remains of other family members, Tsindacaiendoua was buried in the earth "in a separate place." This was likely a plot of ground outside the village palisade that Brébeuf consecrated so that it could be used for the burials of the French and baptized Wendats. The solemn Christian funeral that Brébeuf led, with its chants and songs and prayers, had the desired effect: "this ceremony attracted upon us the eyes of the whole village, and caused several to desire that we should honor their burial in the same way."[20]

One of the people attracted to Christian burial was Joutaya, the man who had received the deathbed visitation from his brother. Joutaya, too ill to leave his longhouse, did not actually witness the Christian funeral, but the reports that were on every tongue piqued his curiosity. He was especially eager to see the priests in the special garb they wore for a funeral. As the dying man told Brébeuf, "he would have been very glad if we had passed through his cabin in the style in which we were dressed, so that he might see us."[21]

It is not known what Brébeuf brought with him to New France, but the Roman Ritual of 1614, an up-to-date guide for those performing such ceremonies, clearly specified what priests presiding over funerals should wear. In addition to the black cassock or robe that Jesuits wore daily, they were supposed to wear a white linen robe over the cassock, a sleeveless purple vestment over that, and another piece of linen around the neck and shoulders. They were also to wear a belt, a silk band around the wrist, and a silk or linen scarf over the shoulders.[22] Wendats, like virtually all peoples, understood the powers of ceremonial dress, and this departure from ordinary priestly garb made quite an impact. Joutaya received his dying wish and was buried in the same separate cemetery as Tsindacaiendoua, in a funeral presided over by the splendidly outfitted Brébeuf.

Separate burial, however, was a double-edged sword. On the one hand, it furthered Brébeuf's agenda by demonstrating that those who accepted baptism were set off from the great mass of Wendats. These "new Christians," as Brébeuf called them (even though they had but the barest knowledge of Christian theology), were special in life and in death, and this was indicated by the physical location of their burials. On the other hand, separate burials reinforced the feeling of many Wendats that accepting baptism entailed an intolerable rejection of their ancestors' ways. In particular, numerous Wendats feared that if they allowed Brébeuf to baptize them, they would not go to the Wendat afterlife and therefore would be separated from the souls of their loved ones.

Later that winter, after the epidemic had subsided and life in Ihonatiria had returned more or less to normal, Brébeuf addressed the issue of the afterlife head-on. His strategy was two-pronged, employing both a carrot and a stick. The carrot involved catechizing children. In the early months of 1635, with the residents of Ihonatiria hunkered down in their longhouses in the depths of the Wendake winter, Brébeuf began to hold group instructional lessons with parents and their children. Attendance was optional, as Brébeuf was hardly in a position to force people to attend, but the meetings were a welcome diversion from the tedium of winter, so numerous villagers came.

Brébeuf signaled the importance of the occasion by putting on a white linen robe over his black one and by donning the flat square cap known as a biretta. He then began to teach. The very first lesson focused on what Brébeuf called a "memorable truth": "that their souls, which are immortal, all go after death either to Paradise or to Hell."[23] The Christian afterlife was the most persuasive aspect of his religion, Brébeuf reasoned, and therefore the best place to start. In subsequent meetings, he asked children the answers to simple questions about the afterlife, and when they responded correctly, he gave them little glass or porcelain beads. These trade items were relatively inexpensive to the Jesuits, but Wendats sought them eagerly because of their continued rarity in Wendake.

Thus did Brébeuf target the youngsters of Ihonatiria for his teachings. Not only were they least set in their ways, but he hoped that their conversion would serve as a carrot—an enticement—for their parents to follow them. This was not because the parents would be convinced by their children's arguments in favor of Christianity; Brébeuf knew too well that Wendat society placed a premium on the opinions of elders and not the mercurial opinions of youths. Rather, Brébeuf played on the Wendat love for their children. As numerous dying Wendat parents pleaded, "We do not wish to be separated from our children, we desire to go to Heaven with them."[24] For those whose children had been catechized and baptized, and had subsequently died, this was a great incentive for the parents to seek baptism for themselves. The potential for a reunion in heaven with their children won over many vacillating Wendats.

The "stick" or corrective aspect of Brébeuf's strategy was to deny the reality of the Wendat afterlife. One example of Brébeuf's use of this technique occurred at a council meeting of all the Bear Nation headmen in April 1636. By this point Brébeuf had lived in Ihonatiria for nearly two years, during which time he had continued to focus on mortuary practices and the afterlife as the surest way to convince Wendats of Christianity's attractions. The headmen invited Brébeuf to the council meeting out of respect for those residents of Ihonatiria who believed in his supernatural powers, but he faced a more skeptical audience than usual. These were individuals from around the Bear Nation who had had few interactions with the Black Robe.

Brébeuf was characteristically undaunted by their skepticism. Rising to face his audience, he told them that "every man, as possessing an immortal soul, would at last, after this life, go to one or the other of two places, Paradise or Hell, and that forever." This they had heard before, but Brébeuf felt that it was crucial to repeat this central component of his message. But Brébeuf did not stop there. Instead, he went on to dismiss traditional Wendat belief in the land of souls. Gaining momentum, he told them that they must choose between the two places "because the matter was decided so far as it concerned all the dead for whom they had made or were going to make feasts; that all those who had slighted God and broken his commandments had followed the path to Hell, where they now were tormented by punishments that could not be imagined."[25] All the rituals the Wendats had performed over the generations, all the farewell feasts and scaffold burials, all the mourning rituals and Feasts of the Dead—all had been for nothing, Brébeuf told them. Their ancestors had angered the Great Voice and were now in hell. The Wendat leaders should embrace Jesus Christ while they still had the chance.

At least one person was deeply moved by these words: a man in his early thirties named Chiwatenhwa. The following year, when he became the Jesuits' most eager student, he would remember that Brébeuf's startling warning initiated his interest in the Black Robes' religion. Soon after the council he presented one of his young sons to Brébeuf "to be baptized, and consequently," as Chiwatenhwa put it, "to go to Heaven."[26]

The rest of the audience was less impressed. Sensing this, and to show that he offered his sharp words in the spirit of friendship, Brébeuf presented the elders with a splendid necklace strung with 1,200 porcelain beads. If single beads given to children for correctly answering catechism questions were appealing, this extraordinary gift must have made quite an impression on the headmen. These beads, if they were unstrung and divided up among the headmen, could be used as status markers, trade items, and ultimately as grave goods and funeral gifts. Still, Brébeuf's contradiction of Wendat beliefs was a much more confrontational strategy than catechizing children. One man stood up and defiantly stated that he wasn't afraid of the tortures of hell. Others, in more characteristic Wendat fashion, simply listened politely to the strange outsider.

But even those unconvinced by Brébeuf's dismissal of their traditions could not ignore the Black Robe altogether. Indeed, this council meeting had been called to determine the time and location of the Bear Nation's next Feast of the Dead, and it was clear that Brébeuf would be invited to the event. Later that spring, as the appointed date of the Feast approached, Brébeuf and the other Jesuits received "several pressing invitations." The Master of the Feast and the headman of the entire Bear Nation urged the Black Robes to attend. "You might have said that the feast would not have been a success without us," Brébeuf inferred from the tone of the entreaties.[27] The Wendats evidently felt that the Black Robes possessed entirely too much supernatural power—not to mention their potential as trading partners, as evidenced by 1,200 beads of porcelain—to be excluded from the event. And with that, preparations began for the great Feast of the Dead.

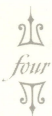

four # The Feast of the Dead

WHEN BRÉBEUF RECEIVED THE INVITATION to attend the Feast of the Dead in May 1636, he was, at long last, linguistically well prepared to make sense of this complex ritual. Years of immersion in the Wendat language, combined with countless hours compiling and studying word lists, allowed Brébeuf to understand even the most nuanced constructions in the Wendat tongue. Just as important, Brébeuf was culturally well prepared to understand the Feast of the Dead. A twenty-first-century North American transported back in time to the 1636 Feast would likely be disgusted by the maggot-filled corpses and perplexed by the elaborate ceremonies centered on human bones. Brébeuf had no such concerns. Like all residents of the early modern world, he knew what death looked and smelled like, having attended numerous deathbed scenes where the effluvia of the dying ran freely, and having witnessed countless funerals where the smell of the decaying body overwhelmed the feeble sprigs of rosemary used to counteract the odor. And like all early modern Catholics, he believed fervently in the power of holy bones. Human remains, he believed, had the ability to heal the lame and cure the sick. Treating bones with complex ritual performances made perfect sense to

Brébeuf. These parallels between Catholic and Wendat beliefs allowed Brébeuf to observe the Feast with great interest and sympathy.

Brébeuf was also impressed by the enormous quantity of material goods used in the Feast and buried in the ossuary: copper kettles, clay pipes, shell beads, and beaver pelts beyond counting. He sometimes worried that the Wendats were impoverishing themselves by offering so many grave goods, but overall he saw this practice as praiseworthy evidence of the Wendat devotion to the souls of the deceased. From today's perspective, the Feast of the Dead's material opulence allows us to understand the Wendat interest in trade with the French—and, by extension, one reason for maintaining good relations with the Black Robes. European goods helped provide comfort and convenience, to be sure, but they also allowed for an unprecedented level of generosity toward residents of the spirit world. At the 1636 Feast, the Wendats enacted an extraordinary display of spiritual and material devotion to the dead.

Such material abundance was not always characteristic of Wendat mortuary customs. In the twelfth and thirteenth centuries, the Iroquoian residents of southern Ontario did not rebury their dead in large ossuaries. Instead, each village seems to have reburied its dead annually in small ossuaries holding between four and thirty individuals. Because the reburials happened every year, and because they involved the dead from only one village, the ossuaries did not need to be very large. The families that gathered to rebury their dead also did not include very many grave goods in the ossuaries, or at least many durable ones such as shell beads and projectile points that would have survived centuries of interment. Most of these burial pits excavated by archaeologists have yielded no artifacts at all.

Starting in the fourteenth century, long before the arrival of Europeans, mortuary customs in the region began to change. Iroquoians of southern Ontario began to practice what might be properly called Feasts of the Dead. Along the northern shore of Lake Ontario, village residents began to wait several years—and perhaps as long as a decade—between reinterments of the dead. Even though the bodies in a given ossuary still seem to have come from only one village, the longer time between reburials meant that the ossuaries were much larger, holding anywhere from one hundred to five hundred individuals. Yet even in these sizable ossuaries very few grave goods have been found. The burial pit known to archaeologists as the Moatfield ossuary, located some seven miles from the shore of Lake Ontario in what is now Toronto, dates to roughly 1300 and held eighty-seven individuals. It contained almost no grave goods other than a turtle effigy pipe. A similar case is the Fairty ossuary, which also dates to the fourteenth century. Despite holding the remains of 512 individuals, this enormous ossuary contained only one stone scraper and a shell bead.

When some of these Iroquoians moved north from Lake Ontario to the land they would call Wendake, they brought their Feast of the Dead ritual with them. As the Bear Nation and Cord-Making Nation coalesced, several villages at a time began to participate in the Feast. At this point the Feast began to symbolize the unity of the villages within a nation. As Gabriel Sagard wrote a century later in the 1620s, "by means of these ceremonies and gatherings they contract new friendships and unions amongst themselves, saying that, just as the bones of their deceased relatives and friends are gathered together and united in one place, so also they themselves ought during their lives to live all together in the same unity and harmony, like good kinsmen and friends."[1] Still, even though the Wendats who attended Feasts of the Dead probably exchanged presents to cement ties of reciprocity, they did not place many durable artifacts into their burial pits. In the Uxbridge ossuary in the heart of Wendake, dug in roughly 1500 for nearly five hundred Wendats, archaeologists found only a few shell beads.

It was not until European goods began to appear in Wendake—at first in a trickle around 1570 through native intermediaries, and after 1609 in a flood with the start of direct trade with the French—that the Wendats began to include large quantities of material offerings in their ossuaries. Interestingly, it was not only European goods that the Wendats placed in ever-greater amounts into their burial pits. Wendats also began to use items of native manufacture such as clay pipes, shell beads, and beaver robes as grave goods. This was partly the result of the fur trade, which brought many native goods to Wendake from other indigenous peoples eager to get their hands on French iron and cloth.

But the increase in goods of native manufacture also resulted from a process that archaeologists call "cultural florescence." This term refers in general to the "flowering" of a culture, which can occur for a variety of reasons. In the case of the Wendats, the arrival of European iron tools allowed for the increased expression of indigenous art forms. With sharp iron awls and knives now at their disposal, Wendat artists fashioned shell beads, ornamental combs, and stone effigy pipes in greater numbers and in finer detail than ever before. While some of these native handicrafts adorned the living, others were given to the dead. The Wendats interpreted their new material wealth within a traditional framework, using their recently acquired European goods and larger numbers of native handicrafts to enhance their long-standing devotion to the deceased.

Thus, when Brébeuf arrived in Wendake, Wendat mortuary customs were continuing the evolution they had begun some five hundred years earlier, albeit at a faster rate of change than before. Brébeuf did not understand this, however, knowing only that it was a great honor to be invited to the 1636 Feast. Unfortunately, the path to the 1636 Feast was strewn with obstacles. In the spring of 1635, the Bear Nation's largest village moved its location in order to be situated on more fertile soil. It had been twelve years since Ossossané had moved, and intensive agriculture and tree cutting had exhausted the surrounding environment. Ossossané's relocation triggered the need for a Feast of the Dead, as residents would no longer be able to keep watch over the old village cemetery.

A Feast was tentatively set for the following year, but in the spring of 1636 divisions arose within the Bear Nation. The split was between the five northern villages of the nation, including Ihonatiria, and the southern villages, including Ossossané. The headmen of the relatively small northern villages complained that they were being shut out of secret councils held by headmen of the larger southern villages, and that they were not receiving their fair share of "presents," presumably from the French to the Bear Nation as a whole.[2] Negotiations ensued between the aggrieved parties, but they could not reach a resolution. The northern villages announced their intention to hold a Feast of the Dead separate from that being planned by Ossossané and the other southern villages.

As the Wendats put it, the kettle was now divided. The Wendats most frequently referred to the reburial ritual as *Yandatsa*, the Kettle, in order to suggest the great feasting that always accompanied the ceremony. It was a term that highlighted the ritual's social component, for to feed one's friends and even strangers out of one's kettle was the characteristic gesture of Wendat hospitality. As Récollet Gabriel Sagard described the Feast of the Dead, "all are made welcome and feasted during the days that the ceremony lasts, and nothing is to be seen there except kettles on the fire, and continual feasting and dancing."[3] From the "kettle" expression the Wendats generated a series of metaphors relating to cookery in order to describe the ritual: to "stir the ashes beneath the kettle" meant to hasten the arrival of the Feast, and to "overturn the kettle" meant to decide against having a Feast. The situation in 1636 was a divided kettle, an image that connoted selfishness rather than the more highly respected trait of generosity.

One might imagine that before the arrival of the French, the kettle was never divided, and that harmony always reigned in determining when and where to hold a Feast of the Dead. In fact, Wendats did occasionally experience conflict in these negotiations, given the powerful meanings ascribed to the ritual. Indeed, one of the Feast's key lessons was that amity within a nation could not be assumed but needed to be worked at: generated and sustained by the ritual commingling of bones. Even though the division was serious, the Wendats assured Brébeuf that it would not lead to the collapse of the Bear Nation. The headmen declared that "in the past there had been similar divisions, which had not ruined" the country.[4]

With the kettle divided, the two antagonistic parties now vied for tangible signs of French allegiance. The token they hoped for: human remains. Two Frenchmen had died in Bear Nation territory since the previous Feast twelve years earlier. The first was Guillaume Chaudron, one of Samuel de Champlain's servants, who died in Ossossané in 1624. The other was Etienne Brûlé, a trader and translator notorious among the Jesuits for his "scandalous" behavior (in particular his multiple native sexual partners), who was murdered in the northern village of Toanché in 1633.[5] Both had been buried in the earth when they died.

The Bear Nation headmen asked Echon to allow them to disinter the Frenchmen's bodies and include their bones in a Feast of the Dead ossuary. The mingling of French and Wendat bones would be a powerful seal of the alliance between the two peoples. But Brébeuf refused, unwilling to allow French Christians—even a scandalous one—to be reburied in unconsecrated ground. He offered a compromise: he would be willing to dig up the Frenchmen's bones and rebury them in a "private grave" near the Feast of the Dead ossuary.[6] The Wendats found this acceptable, but it begged the question: near which ossuary? Now that the kettle was divided there would be two burial pits, one in the north and one in the south. The headmen pressed Brébeuf to decide where the Frenchmen would be reburied, but he astutely deflected the question back to them. An argument broke out between the Bear Nation factions, and a resolution seemed unlikely. Everyone finally decided that the path of least resistance would be to forget the issue. The French bodies remained where they were.

Even though nothing was resolved, the quarrel reveals the degree to which the Wendats were incorporating the French within traditional frameworks. The Wendats had long used the Feast to cement friendships not only within their community but also between themselves and outsiders. Indeed, some of these invited outsiders, including Algonquian groups such as the Nipissings, were so impressed by the ritual that they began holding their own Feasts of the Dead starting in roughly 1640. The Wendats similarly hoped to seal their alliance with the French by asking them to bury their bones in a Wendat ossuary. The headmen were probably stung by Brébeuf's refusal to accept their proposal, but they settled for the second-best symbol of alliance: the presence of Brébeuf and the other Jesuits at the Feast about to be held in Ossossané.

Despite the division of the kettle, numerous families from the northern village of Ihonatiria participated in the southern Feast at Ossossané. They most likely wanted to rebury individuals who had been born in Ossossané but had moved north when they had gotten married. As a result, when the headmen announced the date of the Ossossané Feast, Ihonatiria became a beehive of activity. Family members—perhaps mostly women, as Sagard indicated—headed out to the village cemetery and asked the keeper of the graves to remove their loved ones' remains from their scaffolds. When the keeper of the graves took down the decomposed bodies, the family members wept copiously, as they felt again "the grief they had on the day of the funeral."[7]

Brébeuf, who came from a society where gravediggers commonly disinterred dry bones and placed them into a charnel house as a secondary burial, admired this unself-conscious expression of love for the deceased. "I was present at the spectacle," Brébeuf wrote, "and willingly invited to it all our servants; for I do not think one could see in the world a more vivid picture or more perfect representation of what man is." In other words, the Wendat handling of corpses reminded them that all humans are mortal, and that in death all are equal, two key themes in seventeenth-century Catholicism. Yes, Brébeuf admitted, French cemeteries and charnel houses with their mingled bones of rich and poor had a similar effect. "But it seems to me that what our Indians do on this occasion touches us still more, and makes us see more closely and apprehend more sensibly our wretched state."[8] This was because the Wendats showed no reluctance to soil their hands while taking care of their loved ones' remains.

When the keeper of the graves brought a corpse to a family, they opened the bark coffin (if it had not yet disintegrated) to see in what condition the body remained. The flesh of those who had died a long time ago had almost completely decomposed, leaving only a bit of parchment-like skin attached to the skeleton. These corpses were easy for family members to prepare for the secondary interment. They scraped off any remaining skin and placed it (along with the original beaver robe in which the person had been buried) into a fire. They then disarticulated the skeleton, meaning that they took the bones apart and arranged them in a bundle in a new beaver bag. Brébeuf remarked on a parallel with French practices: "what winding sheets and shrouds are in France, beaver robes are here."[9]

More recently buried bodies, by contrast, writhed with maggots. These would not be disarticulated, but family members still tenderly cared for them. Brébeuf described the corpse of one old man who had died the previous autumn but whose body had begun to decompose only in the last month with the return of springtime warmth: "the worms were swarming all over it, and the corruption that oozed out of it gave forth an almost intolerable stench; and yet they had the courage to take away the robe in which it was enveloped, cleaned it as well as they could, taking the matter off by handfuls, and put the body into a fresh mat and robe, and all this without showing any horror at the corruption." Brébeuf greatly admired the Wendat willingness to treat the dead with such compassion. He took the opportunity to lecture his readers in France. "Is not that a noble example to inspire Christians, who ought to have thoughts much more elevated to acts of charity and works of mercy towards their neighbor?"[10] Brébeuf hoped that the example of the Wendats would motivate French readers to offer better care for the dying and dead.

For the Wendats this ritual preparation of bones had profound meaning, reflected in the linguistic connection between the words for bones, *atisken*, and souls, *esken*. Wendats believed that each person had two souls, which stayed with the body in the village cemetery until the Feast of the Dead. The ritual power of the Feast allowed one of the souls to separate from the body and begin the journey to Aataentsic's village of souls. The other remained in or near the ossuary unless reborn as an infant Wendat. Therefore, the Wendats who cleaned the bones so tenderly were preparing to release their loved ones' souls to the afterlife. It was a moment of powerful connection between the living and the spirit world.

When the residents of Ihonatiria had finished disarticulating the dried skeletons and cleaning the corpses of those who had died more recently, they carried the fresh beaver-wrapped bundles into their longhouses, where each family staged a small feast to honor the dead. Next, the village headman held a feast of souls to honor a previous headman who was about to be reburied. The village rang with songs and chants, including the "cry of souls," *haéé haé*, simultaneously mournful and cathartic.

Finally, it was time to head to Ossossané for the Feast of the Dead. The ceremony was scheduled to begin Saturday, May 10, according to the French calendar. We do not know why the Wendats chose early May for this Feast. In other years the ritual may have occurred at various times throughout the warmer months; the 1636 Feast is the only one for which we know the date. Yet it seems likely that the Wendats chose this time frame in light of practical and symbolic connections with the seasonal calendar. Early May was just prior to planting season, so it was the last moment before the Wendats would be busy tending their crops. It was also a richly symbolic moment when the earth once again came alive after the snowbound Wendake winter: the first edible fern shoots peeked through the forest's leaf litter, the mighty northern pike began to spawn, and early wildflowers bloomed white and red and yellow. In western Europe, warmer than Wendake as a result of the effects of the North Atlantic Current, the primary religious celebration of renewal (Easter) occurred between late March and late April in order to coincide with spring and planting and their obvious connections to rebirth. It is possible that the Wendats used a similar logic when scheduling their most important ritual about death and the afterlife in the month whose Wendat name meant "one plants or sows."[11]

So on roughly May 1, the villagers gathered up their bone bundles and partly decayed corpses and headed toward Ossossané. Ordinarily this 12-mile walk could be accomplished in a day, but the procession had an important social component. The Ihonatiria residents stopped at villages along the way, picking up others headed to Ossossané, and spending the night in the longhouses of friends and family members. Sharing food and lodging must have gone a long way toward repairing the breach between the northern and southern headmen, or perhaps the ordinary villagers did not pay much heed to the headmen's quarrels. Either way, it was three days of bittersweet feasting and walking—remembering the dead and celebrating the living—before the Ihonatiria residents reached Ossossané on about May 3.

The people streaming into Ossossané from all over Wendake were housed in the old village location, where several longhouses still stood. And even though the Wendats were preparing for a burial ritual, one should not imagine that the week leading up to the Feast was all sadness and solemnity. The French term for this ritual, *Fête des Morts*, might more accurately be translated into modern English as Festival of the Dead, which better suggests the festivities that accompanied the gathering.

Indeed, old Ossossané took on the atmosphere of a country fair. Day after day new processions arrived, some with two or three hundred people carrying their bone bundles. The temporary housing buzzed with the excitement of friendships renewed and new acquaintances made. Everyone joined in games of skill. Over here women competed in shooting arrows; closest to a target won a prize of a porcupine belt or a string of porcelain beads. Over there young men displayed their marksmanship by shooting arrows at a stick. Whoever could hit the slender target won an axe, a knife, or even a beaver robe. And of course, because this was the great *Yandatsa* or Kettle, everywhere one looked clay and copper cooking vessels were filled to overflowing with deer and dogs and *sagamité*.

The ceremony was supposed to begin on May 10, but bad weather forced a postponement until May 12. By that point some two thousand people had arrived from around the Bear Nation and beyond. At about noon on the appointed day, the Jesuits and the others lodged in old Ossossané walked a mile to the burial pit. Brébeuf was staggered by the size of the ritual platform and ossuary. He compared the size of the whole area to the Place Royale in Paris, an opulent square surrounded by tall buildings. He reported that the ossuary itself was a circular pit ten feet deep and almost thirty feet in diameter. Around the pit, he wrote, there was a well-built scaffold about fifty feet in diameter and nine or ten feet high, with additional poles and cross-poles on top of that, from which the Wendats would hang bone bundles and presents. It was a remarkable physical testament to the Wendat respect for the dead.

But how do we know that Brébeuf wasn't exaggerating to impress his French readers? We know because in 1947 and 1948 archaeologists from the Royal Ontario Museum of Archaeology (now the Royal Ontario Museum or ROM) excavated the very ossuary where Brébeuf and thousands of Wendats stood more than three hundred years earlier. This excavation, under the supervision of archaeologist Kenneth E. Kidd, did not involve the descendants of the Wendats in any way. In what was standard practice of the period, Wendats were not consulted or asked for permission. As a result, this excavation—and the three hundred boxes of human remains it produced—would become controversial in later decades. But at the time, scholars around the globe hailed the excavation of the Ossossané ossuary as a model of cutting-edge scientific archaeology.

By the 1940s Euro-Americans had been digging up Wendat ossuaries for over a century. In the early 1800s, white farmers began to move into the area that had been known as Wendake but was now part of Upper Canada (and would eventually become southern Ontario). As they readied their fields for spring planting, these farmers occasionally plowed up large bone caches. Some people were curious and collected the arrowheads or shell beads they found; others simply cursed the pit for making it hard to plant crops over it.

In 1848 a British Army surgeon named Edward Bawtree published the first attempt at a scientific account of these burial pits in the *Edinburgh New Philosophical Journal*. Realizing the value of the ossuaries for understanding the Amerindians who had earlier inhabited the region, Bawtree described as carefully as he could the contents of four Wendat ossuaries ranging from nine to fifteen feet in diameter. The Wendats dug these burial pits after the arrival of European goods, as indicated by the presence of brass kettles, iron axes, and iron cups. In the decades following Bawtree's publication, amateur archaeologists and looters found dozens of other Wendat ossuaries, some of which were described in print, but most of which were merely raided for the artifacts they held. Despite all this interest, no one had managed to identify the ossuary from the 1636 Feast of the Dead.

Intrigued by this mystery, amateur archaeologist Frank Ridley began after World War II to search for Ossossané, both the village and the ossuary. In 1946 he thought he had found what he was looking for and contacted Kenneth Kidd at the ROM for confirmation. Kidd excitedly reported that he believed this was indeed Ossossané, so he immediately began to plan for a full-scale excavation. Kidd's budget for a six-week dig in 1947 was a modest $2,773, which would cover the cost of eight people digging and cataloguing findings, a cook, and a team of horses to cart away dirt.

The crew began its work on July 2, 1947. Kidd was joined by his wife, Martha, who performed numerous important roles including photographer and drafter of field drawings, and several museum staff members, including Kidd's assistants Audrey Lucas and Vera Clark. In photographs taken that summer the crew appears uniformly happy, despite the hard work and hot conditions. The young women—Kidd, Lucas, and Clark—seem to have especially enjoyed the responsibilities they shouldered at a time when professional archaeologists were almost all male. Word of their excitement got back to the museum, and on July 22 staff member Joan Hay wrote a letter to Kenneth Kidd asking if she could leave her secretarial job and join the excavation for a week. Kidd granted permission and Hay hurried to Ossossané.

Instead of merely digging up the ossuary and counting the native and European artifacts, as earlier generations had done, Kidd's team followed the latest scientific methods of professional archaeology. It was fairly obvious where the ossuary lay: in three centuries the bones had settled, leaving a saucer-shaped depression in the ground of a diameter that strongly suggested a burial pit. Still, the archaeologists proceeded carefully, digging a test trench to determine the depth and boundaries of the ossuary. That accomplished, they began to mark off the area for further excavation. Kidd described the rigorous procedures they followed: "Work . . . was begun by laying out the surrounding half acre in five foot squares. Contours were noted and excavation by 3 inch levels was begun. Photographs, profiles and square plans were made wherever necessary; the locations of artifacts were accurately noted, and the objects removed with all possible care, cleaned, catalogued, and packed for shipping."[12]

The "excavation by 3 inch levels" was an especially important aspect of the scientific approach to archaeology. This allowed the investigators to understand relationships: both chronological (which objects were placed into the pit first) and spatial (which artifacts were placed next to particular human remains). Kidd's field notes, preserved at the ROM, indicate just how carefully his team observed these standards.

The six-week digging season in 1947 proved too brief to excavate such a large area so painstakingly. The team therefore returned the following summer and spent another six weeks removing and cataloguing bones and artifacts. Kidd then set about making sense of an enormous quantity of data: hundreds of artifacts and thousands of bones and bone fragments. Five years later his findings were accepted for publication by *American Antiquity*, the leading North American archaeology journal.

The evidence Kidd presented corroborated Brébeuf's account of the Feast. The investigators found that the burial pit measured twenty-four feet across, only slightly smaller than Brébeuf's estimate. Surrounding the pit they discovered dozens of post molds: circular soil disturbances that showed where wooden posts had been driven into the ground. The post molds ranged from six to twelve inches in diameter, averaging about nine inches. These substan-

Archaeologists at Ossossané. Kenneth Kidd, Frank Ridley, Audrey Lucas, and Vera Clark investigate the test trench on July 14, 1947. Here the archaeologists attempt to determine the extent of the ossuary and its surrounding platform. They appear to be enjoying themselves despite the hot sun. With permission of the Royal Ontario Museum © ROM, detail of item A.4.7.

tial timbers supported the platform surrounding the ossuary; the post molds indicated that the platform was about fifty-five feet in diameter, even larger than Brébeuf thought. It was truly an enormous structure.

Most of Kidd's analysis focused on the grave goods of both European and native manufacture, confirming Brébeuf's report that the Wendats expressed their devotion to the dead through material offerings. Kidd found European iron goods such as knives, awls, scissors, and an iron key. It is unknown whether the Wendats invested the key with the metaphorical meanings it held for Europeans, who might have seen it as unlocking a door to the afterlife. Kidd unearthed two pipes of native manufacture, one of which was a beautiful vase-shaped pipe bowl made of green serpentine. The ossuary also held numerous objects of personal adornment. Kidd counted 998 beads, including 656 made of shell, 313 of glass, 16 of copper, and 13 of catlinite, a brownish-red stone prized for its workability. Kidd's team also found six copper finger rings, two of them still on finger bones. One of these was a signet ring of a type favored by Jesuits and referred to by archaeologists as a "Jesuit ring." Is it too far-fetched to wonder whether Brébeuf had worn the ring and given it to a favored Wendat who showed interest in Christianity? Such speculation was not Kidd's style; his article contains no suggestion of this.

Curiously, Kidd was relatively uninterested in the human remains, certainly less interested in bones than the Wendat participants and Catholic observers of the 1636 Feast. As Kidd wrote, "judging by the volume of the bone mass, it would appear that the pit must have contained close to 1000 skeletons; however, no count has yet been made to ascertain the exact number."[13] Kidd's inattention to the bones stemmed partly from the overwhelming amount of confusing data they generated, and partly from Kidd's lack of training as an osteoarchaeologist, one who specializes in the analysis of bones. It may also have resulted in part from the team's lack of Wendat input; had Amerindians been involved from the start, they almost certainly would have wanted the bones analyzed and reburied promptly.

Instead, the bones began a journey of five decades and hundreds of miles as several teams of scientists measured them and scrutinized them under microscopes. About half the bones were sent in 1949 to Philadelphia, where two scientists studied them to learn about the health of the Wendat population. By 1972 the bones had been returned to Ontario, where a University of Toronto researcher and his doctoral students performed much more in-depth analyses of the human remains.

These studies in the 1970s and 1980s produced a great deal of information about the Wendats buried in the Ossossané ossuary. Most basically, investigators determined a "minimum number of individuals" (MNI), which is more difficult than it sounds given that the bones had all been mixed together in the ossuary. Researchers counted each different kind of bone they found: so many thigh bones, so many fifth vertebrae. The largest number of any one kind of bone represents the MNI. In this case they found 681 right ilia (one of the

Green Serpentine Pipe Bowl. A stem was inserted into the hole on the right side for drawing out the smoke. The hole at the bottom was for a cord that was used to suspend the pipe from the user's neck or a storage hook. The graceful curves, striking color, and smooth feel of this item of native manufacture made it aesthetically pleasing and therefore worthy of burial with the dead. With permission of the Royal Ontario Museum © ROM, item 949.129.15.

bones of the pelvis), which meant that there were at least 681 Wendats reburied at the 1636 Feast. Furthermore, based on the skeletons that were in good enough condition to allow the sex of the individual to be determined, scientists found a male:female ratio of 0.94:1.00, that is, for every ninety-four men there were one hundred women. This slightly skewed ratio suggests that more

Copper Signet Ring. Jesuits frequently wore this type of ring, with the IHS symbol of the Society of Jesus engraved on the signet. Is it possible that it once belonged to Jean de Brébeuf? With permission of the Royal Ontario Museum © ROM, item 947.129.24.

men than women died violent deaths. As we have seen, Wendats buried such individuals in the earth and did not rebury them in the communal ossuary.

Comparison with other Wendat ossuaries showed the effects of the epidemics that began to ravage the Bear Nation in 1634. Scientists calculated the life expectancy at birth for those buried in Ossossané at only twenty-one years. This compares with a life expectancy based on earlier ossuaries (from the years 1300 to 1600) of thirty to thirty-three years. And whereas the burial pits from previous centuries indicated that 60 to 70 percent of children lived to the age of fifteen, that figure declined to 40 percent for the Wendats buried in Ossossané. This was a remarkably swift change in the population's demographic profile: the ossuary held those who had died from 1624 to 1636, but epidemics had struck the Wendats only since 1634.

Despite the scientific and historical interest in figures such as these, the decision to analyze the Ossossané bones for five decades without Wendat input came back to haunt the ROM. As the Wendats at the 1636 Feast might have told Kidd and his successors, it is a mistake to underestimate the spiritual power of human remains.

That was a sentiment Brébeuf likewise heartily endorsed as he watched the Feast begin on May 12, 1636. He was deeply impressed by the way that the Wendats invested human remains with spiritual and emotional significance. When the Feast commenced at midday, men and women carried their loved ones' bones to the edge of the burial pit, unwrapped the beaver bundles, and, with tears streaming down their cheeks, said a final farewell to the deceased.

This was clearly a powerful moment for the participants; Brébeuf was similarly moved: "I admired the tenderness of one woman toward her father and children." This woman's father, a highly respected leader, had died at a good old age. Brébeuf reported that "she combed his hair and handled his bones, one after the other, with as much affection as if she would have desired to restore life to him." She was just as loving with the bones of her little children: "she put on their arms bracelets of porcelain and glass beads, and bathed their bones with her tears." Using the European trade goods that had become increasingly common in Wendake, this woman shared a physical intimacy with her family members' bones that some modern readers find surprising, yet which Brébeuf "admired."[14]

Brébeuf's admiration stemmed from Catholicism's long veneration of holy bones. Catholics since late antiquity had invested the bones of the "very special dead" with supernatural powers, and the Catholic missionaries who came to the New World were no exception to this.[15] Brébeuf would not have considered the bones of the Wendat woman's family members to be as powerful as the relics of Christian saints, but he understood the woman's general impulse.

To get a sense of the attitudes toward bones that French priests and nuns brought with them to New France, witness the intense engagement of Quebec nun Marie de l'Incarnation with the bones of her fellow nun and missionary, Marie de Saint-Joseph. In 1663 Marie de l'Incarnation described the ecstasy she experienced when opening the coffin of her dear friend. The coffin had to be moved in order to make way for a chapel they were building, so the nuns of the convent took the opportunity "to see in what state her body then was." Fearing corruption and decay—the young woman had been dead eleven years—they instead "found all her flesh consumed and changed into a milk-white paste of about a finger's depth." The heart, brains, and bones were all in their proper place, "the whole without any ill odor." This was a delightful sight. "The moment we opened the coffin we were filled with a joy and sweetness so great that I cannot express it to you." Before reburying their deceased companion, the women decided to wash the bones. "The hands of those who touched them smelled of an odor like irises. The bones were as if oily, and when they had been washed and dried, our hands and the linens had the same odor." Touching these bones did not fill these women with fear and dread, but, similar to the Wendat woman's experience, "they filled us rather with feelings of union and love for the deceased."[16]

Brébeuf also believed that the remains of particularly holy individuals had special powers. He brought saints' bones with him to New France to use when other forms of supernatural intervention such as prayer seemed ineffective. Just a few months before the Feast of the Dead, Brébeuf had an opportunity to demonstrate his skills as a healer when a woman struggled with a difficult childbirth. Ordinarily, Wendat women gave birth without a great deal of obvious pain; their culture promoted a stoic approach to pain of all sorts, including labor. But this time something was wrong. Twenty-four hours of labor had passed and still the baby would not come. The turning point? When Echon employed a holy bone. The woman "brought forth a child happily, as soon as we had applied to her a relic of Our Blessed Father St. Ignatius," the founder of the Jesuits.[17] Brébeuf may have explained to the woman and her companions that the bone was not magical, and that it merely served as a conduit for asking St. Ignatius to intercede with Christ in heaven. But the lesson the Wendats likely took away from this dramatic event was that Catholics, like the Wendats themselves, invested human remains with supernatural power.

This belief was clear as the Feast continued and ceremonial leaders gently pulled the tearful woman away from the remains of her father and children. Now came the time to display the presents—for both the dead and the living—that people had brought with them. The two thousand participants divided themselves by village and by family and then hung their presents from the cross-poles on the scaffolding surrounding the ossuary. They displayed beaver robes and other gifts that included European items such as glass beads, iron knives, and copper kettles—roughly 1,200 items in all, according to Brébeuf. All the participants brought presents to Ossossané; even relatively poor Wendats "bring and leave there whatever they have most valuable, and suffer much, in order not to appear less liberal [i.e., generous] than the others in this celebration. Every one makes it a point of honor."[18]

The Wendats exhibited these presents for two hours "to give strangers time to see the wealth and magnificence of the country."[19] These "strangers" included non-Wendat groups such as the Nipissings, who had long attended Feasts of the Dead as honored guests, and also Brébeuf and the other Jesuits and French servants who joined him. The Wendats were clearly proud of their material wealth, which had increased so much since the start of the fur trade with the French. They were just as proud of the way they used this wealth to cement good relations with the dead and the living.

At about three o'clock in the afternoon everyone took down their presents from the display poles and repacked the goods into beaver robes. Then came a signal from the leaders of the ritual: it was time to hang the bone bundles from the scaffolding. This was a crucial moment in the ritual and people jockeyed for the best positions on the scaffold: they scrambled toward the platform, "running as if to the assault of a town."[20] Hundreds of people climbed the ladders to the platform and hung their bone bundles—still wrapped in beaver robes—from the same cross-poles from which they had recently suspended the presents.

Most people then descended from the platform, but a few leaders stayed on the scaffold and spent the next several hours announcing each of the presents. Brébeuf stated that these gifts were offered "in the name of the dead to certain specified persons." But when he quoted what the leaders actually said, a slightly different meaning emerges. "This," the leaders said, holding up a gift, "is what such and such a dead man gives to such and such a relative."[21] It seems that the Wendats did not think a gift was given *in the name of* the dead but rather by the dead person himself, by which they perhaps meant that from the afterworld the deceased's spirit influenced the giving of the present.

While this was going on, others lined the burial pit with beaver robes. These individuals covered the bottom and sides of the pit with forty-eight robes. At ten beaver pelts per robe, this represented yet more evidence of the Wendats' material devotion to the dead. The ossuary was now properly prepared to receive its first corpses. Ten or twelve Wendats began to place the whole bodies—the individuals who had died too recently to be disarticulated—at the bottom of the pit. Rather than the solemn procedure one might imagine, this stage in the ritual generated a "din of confused voices" as some people called out directions and others did not listen.[22] Order was restored when the bodies were finally arranged at the bottom of the pit. The Wendats placed three copper kettles into the very center, perhaps to connect with their name for the ritual: *Yandatsa*, the Kettle. With night falling, this was the last ritual activity of the Feast's first day. The Wendats spent the night in the vicinity of the ossuary, building fires, setting up kettles, and sharing food with one another. Brébeuf and the other French observers opted to walk the mile back to old Ossossané to spend the night there.

Brébeuf and the others awoke at daybreak and were just about to begin their journey back to the ossuary when they heard a horrible roaring of voices in the distance. They hurried as fast as they could to the pit, where they found a scene of terrible confusion. It turned out that while the Wendats slept one of the bone bundles fell from the scaffold into the pit, making a loud noise and awakening everyone nearby. Brébeuf explained that the bundle was likely "not securely tied, or was perhaps too heavy for the cord that fastened it." But the Wendats may have taken this unusual occurrence as a sign from the supernatural world, for everyone then rushed to the scaffold to begin dumping the bones into the pit. Five or six people stood in the pit, arranging the bones with poles, as everyone else emptied their beaver bags and tossed the bones in. Again the air resounded with "confused voices."[23]

Brébeuf found disconcerting the level of chaos he witnessed on both the first and second days of the Feast as Wendats placed bodies and bones into the ossuary. He was used to Catholic rituals in Europe that were highly scripted and controlled: there was a rubric to follow, endorsed by bishops and enforced by priests. The Wendats had no such centralized mechanism for imposing uniformity in ritual practice across time and space. There was a Master of the Feast, but he ruled more by consensus than fiat, in the manner of Wendat political leaders. If the people decided that a fallen bundle signaled the moment to fill the pit with bones, there was little he or anyone else could do about it.

As the participants continued to empty the bundles into the pit, they began to sing, in voices that Brébeuf found "sorrowful and lugubrious."[24] Soon the Wendats had finished depositing the remains of their loved ones and the ossuary was filled with bones and grave goods to within two feet of the ossuary's rim. The beaver robes lining the sides of the pit were now folded over the mass of bones, and the rest of the pit was filled with mats, bark, and sand. Finally, in an apparent offering to the spirits of the dead, perhaps to aid them in their long journey to Aataentsic's village of souls, women brought dishes of corn and laid them atop the ossuary. All that remained was for the living to give presents to one another, as a final way to cement ties across lineages and villages. The Feast of the Dead, anticipated for twelve years, was complete.

For everyone except Brébeuf, that is. He was disturbed that the ossuary held the bones of fifteen or twenty of what he called "Christians," Wendats who had received baptism before they died. As nominal Christians they should have been buried in consecrated ground. So Brébeuf and the other Jesuits "said for their souls a *De profundis*," the Latin name for Psalm 130, which begins, "Out of the depths have I cried unto thee, O Lord." This is a psalm that expresses hope in the efficacy of prayer, so Brébeuf prayed that "this feast will cease, or will be only for Christians, and will take place with ceremonies as sacred as the ones we saw are foolish and useless."[25]

At last, at the end of a long and largely sympathetic account of the Feast, Brébeuf revealed his true colors. His perspective was not akin to that of a modern anthropologist, who records the details of rituals for value-neutral ends, but of a missionary with one goal in mind: conversion. Brébeuf cried to his god because, even though he "admired" aspects of the Feast and used the Wendats as a model to inspire French Christians to greater devotion to the dead, the ritual was ultimately "foolish and useless," a "picture of Hell," evidence of how far the Wendats would have to travel before they were, in Brébeuf's eyes, good Christians.[26]

Yet Brébeuf's hope for the future deserves careful scrutiny. Yes, he thought this ritual might someday cease. But he also held out another possibility: that the Feast of the Dead would be "only for Christians," with "sacred" Christian ceremonies. Imagine that future: Christian Wendats bury their dead on scaffolds, periodically scrape the deceased's bones and place them into beaver bundles, bring them to a large ossuary for secondary interment, and offer prayers to the Christian god, the Great Voice. The only difference would be in the final step. Brébeuf had no problem with the Wendat practices associated with burial, corpse preparation, and reburial. In fact, rather than tearing down Wendat deathways and starting over, Brébeuf hoped to build on their already existing—and already powerful, as he readily acknowledged—mortuary practices.

In this Brébeuf followed the lead of more than a millennium of missionary efforts within Europe and elsewhere. As Christianity spread from its starting point as a small sect along the Mediterranean to far-flung areas such as Ireland and Denmark, it built on the deathways of non-Christians—literally. In Flonheim in what is now Germany, for example, eighth-century Christians constructed a church directly over a non-Christian cemetery. The non-Christian Franks in this region performed "row burials" that symbolically linked living and dead members of the clan. When Christians erected a church above these row burials, they essentially gave their ancestors Christian burials after the fact. They also highlighted a crucial similarity between the Christians and non-Christians: both believed that the dead were, in effect, important members of society who exerted influence on the living. The earlier row burials and later church burials both placed the dead at the center of the community's spiritual life.

Brébeuf's vision of a Christian Feast of the Dead likewise flowed from essential similarities between Catholic and Wendat religions: both viewed mortuary rituals as key moments for interacting with the supernatural world, and, most importantly, both viewed human remains as having powerful spiritual significance. These parallels, however, did not lead Brébeuf to the conclusion that Wendats should continue to practice the Feast as they always had. Rather, Brébeuf hoped to use these similarities to ease the transition to a new Christian Feast. This would take hard work, so Brébeuf and the other Jesuits headed back to Ihonatiria, reenergized in their mission to Christianize Wendake's native people.

The Wendats, on the other hand, headed to their various villages, hoping to resume life as usual, yet after the Feast it is likely that they were especially cognizant of the connections between the dead and the living. Once home the women would begin the hard yet vital work of planting the year's crops. Seeds, like bones, are the hard and seemingly lifeless remains of previously living matter. After the Feast of the Dead, the women of Wendake dug tiny pits and buried their seeds in the earth, prayed to their gods, and waited for new life to spring from the sandy soil.

five

Epidemic Tensions

AFTER THE WOMEN OF WENDAKE dug their seed burial pits in the second half of May 1636, they settled into a familiar summer routine. When the corn was a few inches high, they hoed the earth into little hills around the bright green stalks and planted beans and squash in the hills. They and their children weeded the fields and chased away hungry pests such as crows and squirrels. The men of Wendake were absent for long stretches, engaged in the usual summer activities of fishing on the great lake and trading with Algonquian hunter-gatherers for thick northern pelts.

This comfortable routine was shattered in early September when disease once again tore through Wendake. Women and men suffered from violent fevers, chills, exhaustion, and stomach cramps caused by what may have been a strep infection that, unknown to the Wendats, originated with the French. Again the Wendats died in horrifying numbers: perhaps 5 to 10 percent of the population, or between one and two thousand individuals, died before the epidemic relented in the spring of 1637.[1]

The Wendats and the French responded similarly to this outbreak of disease. Both groups mobilized their most potent healing powers to combat the pestilence. Both called on the supernatural world to end the dying. And both viewed the epidemic as an opportunity to convince the other group of the superiority of its own healing magic. Yet only the French hoped to use this supernatural contest over death and life to convert the other group to its own religious system. In the wake of the Feast of the Dead, Brébeuf and the other Jesuits believed they had to reform the "foolish and useless" Wendat death-ways. An abundance of death gave them the chance to put their strategies into action.

Before they could do so, the Jesuits had to get back on their feet, for this epidemic was unique in that it struck the French as hard as the Wendats. Strep infections are caused by bacteria, which do not confer lifelong immunity, unlike viral illnesses such as measles and smallpox, so the French were just as vulnerable as their Wendat counterparts. The Jesuits perceived a silver lining in this: because they too were sick, the Wendats could not accuse them of deliberately causing the disease, as they had in 1634. But this was only a small comfort to the Jesuits. For a time it seemed that the sickness might put an end to the Christian mission in Wendake.

Father Isaac Jogues was the first Frenchman to succumb to the disease. On September 17 he showed signs of sickness, mild symptoms at first, but daily his fever grew increasingly violent. A few days later, one of the Jesuits' servants became ill, and then another. Brébeuf, who remained healthy, nursed them. He gave them raisins and prunes, brought all the way from France for their alleged medicinal qualities. He prepared soup with duck and wild herbs such as purslane, whose thick fleshy leaves were used in Europe for healing. When the Jesuits' hen was in the right mood and laid an egg, Brébeuf offered that. And, of course, he prayed with the sick men. Ominously, Jogues showed no signs of improvement in spite of Brébeuf's ministrations. Indeed, Jogues's condition went from bad to worse as he began to bleed "copiously" and "persistently" from the nose.[2] For two days nothing could stop the bleeding.

Brébeuf prescribed a remedy that today seems bizarre, or at the very least counterintuitive: bloodletting. With poor Jogues bleeding profusely from the nose for two days, why on earth would Brébeuf demand that more blood be drained from his system? Because in the humoral theory that dominated European medical thought, illness resulted from an imbalance of humors. A bloody nose indicated that an *excess* of blood caused this mysterious malady, so bloodletting was the obvious course of action.

All of the Jesuits had some training as physicians, but because Brébeuf was among the few healthy Frenchmen, and because he shouldered the extra responsibility of being the mission's Father Superior, he stepped forward to perform the procedure. No description exists of Brébeuf's bloodletting technique, but it is likely that he employed the standard practices of his time. If so, he tightly bound one of Jogues's arms with a tourniquet to bring the veins closer to the skin's surface. Then Brébeuf gripped between his thumb and forefinger a lancet, a small two-sided blade, less than two inches long and half an inch wide, which was for centuries so closely associated with physicians that today a prestigious medical journal is entitled *The Lancet*. Brébeuf pushed the point of his blade lengthwise into Jogues's vein—never crosswise, or he might sever the vein entirely—and then quickly pulled it out. This made an incision of between one-eighth and one-quarter of an inch, which allowed the blood to flow freely into a bowl. Brébeuf probably hoped to drain a full pint of blood, the usual amount in cases such as this. When the bowl was full, Brébeuf bandaged his patient to stop the flow.

Brébeuf proved himself a skilled healer, in the eyes of the French. Later that day Jogues's nose finally stopped bleeding, and the next day his fever began to abate. The bloodletting and prayers seemed to have done the trick. In the following weeks Brébeuf would bleed his French companions several more times, almost always with similarly "favorable" outcomes.[3]

We can only imagine how the residents of Ihonatiria interpreted this bloody healing rite. Wendats almost certainly witnessed the procedure; several times the Jesuits complained about the frequent "visits and importunities" of the Wendats, who watched with curiosity the proceedings within the Jesuits' little longhouse. One Jesuit wrote that the Wendats "wondered at" French healing practices in general, but we do not know what they thought of bloodletting in particular.[4] However, they must have interpreted French healing in light of their own customs, which were in some ways similar to the practices they watched Brébeuf perform. Like the French, the Wendats used herbs they gathered in the fields and forests to heal the sick. They also understood the role of the healer, and they expected such individuals to make supernatural incantations the way that Echon beseeched his god, the Great Voice, to cure the sick men.

Even bloodletting had parallels among the Wendats, who believed that the flow of blood had supernatural connections. For this reason, as a Wendat man put it, "when we wish to have success in hunting . . . we cut and slash our bodies, so that the blood runs down abundantly." Wendats also connected the release of blood with healing. Gabriel Sagard reported in the 1620s that a Wendat healer, when working on a patient, usually "blows upon the place where the pain is, makes incisions, [and] sucks out the corrupted blood." They also, in order to "purge out the corrupt humor of swellings . . . make incisions and cuts, with small sharp stones, into the fat of their legs."[5] Like Europeans, Wendats believed that blood had powerful associations with health, and their healers performed procedures to remove blood from ailing patients.

These parallels led Brébeuf to see healing as a supernatural contest. He used the similarities between French and Wendat practices to communicate with Ihonatiria's residents on their own terms: indeed, several Wendats asked Brébeuf to bleed them, which he eagerly did. But Brébeuf also hoped to use what he believed to be the superiority of French healing to convince the Wendats of the superiority of the Christian god. For this reason Brébeuf had written the previous year, "if some wise and upright physician would come here, he would perform noble cures for their souls, in relieving their bodies." That is, a skilled French physician who could cure the Wendats' ailments would also help convert them to Catholicism by demonstrating the Great Voice's power over life and death. Brébeuf was frustrated that whenever he asserted that Wendat healing was nothing but hocus-pocus, the Wendats responded by saying, "Well then, you cure us."[6] Brébeuf longed for a fully trained French doctor to come to Wendake, but in the meantime he would have to play that role.

This he did with great gusto as the Jesuits and their servants continued to fall ill. Father Pierre Chastellain came down with a burning fever that made him terribly restless. He could barely sleep on the Wendat-style bed of reeds and bark that all the Jesuits used in their longhouse. Father Charles Garnier was the next to be struck by the fever. Brébeuf twice tried to bleed Garnier, but the blood would not flow; perhaps Brébeuf wished more than ever for a real physician skilled in the art of bloodletting. A hired Frenchman referred to in the sources only as Dominique became so sick that Brébeuf performed the sacrament of extreme unction or holy anointing.

Again we do not have a description of this performance, but because extreme unction was a carefully scripted ritual, we can be fairly sure of what Brébeuf did. With some Wendats likely looking on, Brébeuf dipped his right thumb in holy oil and anointed Dominique in the form of a cross on his eyelids, his ear lobes, both nostrils, his closed lips, his palms, and finally the soles of both feet. As he performed these actions, Brébeuf intoned in Latin,

"Through this holy anointing and through His tender mercy may the Lord forgive thee whatever sins thou hast committed by the sense of sight," and by the sense of hearing, and so on through "the power of walking."[7] This was undoubtedly a compelling scene for the Wendats who witnessed it, with the French holy man offering his solemn incantations while touching the gravely ill man tenderly and intimately. And perhaps it helped convince some that Brébeuf was indeed a supernatural healer, as Dominique eventually returned from the brink of death and made a full recovery.

Brébeuf presided over another sacrament for the sick, but this one may have been kept from the eyes of curious Wendats. Daily during the epidemic, Brébeuf or another priest performed the sacrament of the Eucharist (Holy Communion) for the ailing Jesuits. Or rather, they performed the ritual nightly, "the Father Superior, or some one else, carrying it [the consecrated bread and wine] to them during the night." By offering the sick Jesuits the body and blood of Christ, Brébeuf greatly fortified their psychological state. As one Jesuit wrote, "it was from this treasure house that they drew so many holy resolutions, and so many pious sentiments, which made them delight in, and tenderly cherish their condition."[8] Receiving the body and blood of Christ was such a powerful supernatural experience that it could make the Jesuits "delight in" their sickness.

But it was also such a powerful ritual that the Jesuits did their best to keep the details of it from the Wendats. Because the Jesuits closed their longhouse to Wendat visitors every evening, the nighttime performance of the ritual likely concealed it from their Wendat hosts. The Jesuits worried that if the Wendats witnessed the French consuming their Savior's body and blood, the Wendats would equate the Eucharist with their own practices of ritual cannibalism, which the Jesuits dearly hoped to stamp out.

This concern long marked the Jesuit mission to the Wendats. From his very first years in Wendake, Brébeuf skated around what Holy Communion actually entailed. When he composed a catechism or question-and-answer instructional dialogue for the Wendats in the 1620s, he translated "Eucharist" into the Wendat word *atonesta*, meaning "one gives recognition, thanks by such a means." This was a bland formulation unlikely to convey the ritual's potency, but it also avoided the explosive suggestion that the French consumed their god's body. As late as 1638 a Jesuit wrote, "we never speak to them about it [the Eucharist] until after a long proof of their faith." Still, the Black Robes may not have been secretive enough in the fall of 1636: soon a rumor spread through Wendake that, as the Jesuits put it, "we have with us a dead body, which serves us as black magic."⁹ Still, Brébeuf would not allow these concerns to dissuade him from presiding over the nightly feast on Christ's body and blood.

Thus through means natural and supernatural did Brébeuf attempt to keep his fellow Frenchmen from death. Slowly, with occasional setbacks, Jogues and Garnier and the others regained their strength. By the middle of October they were able to eat *sagamité*. And by the middle of November they joined Brébeuf in assisting sick Wendats, which was necessary because the epidemic lasted much longer among the region's indigenous residents. Even as the Jesuits returned to full health, the Wendats watched in horror as the disease spread to all corners of their homeland. In the fall and winter of 1636–1637, Brébeuf had no shortage of patients in the longhouses of Ihonatiria.

But Brébeuf, of course, was not the only supernatural healer in Wendake. And Brébeuf was not the only person who viewed healing as a contest between rival gods. Wendake's most influential shaman, a hunchbacked and "extremely misshapen" little man named Tonnerawanont, journeyed to Ihonatiria in October 1636 to demonstrate that his magic was more powerful than that of the Jesuits. Tonnerawanont, who could make "entire villages bend to his decrees," took great pride in his accomplishments as a healer and did not hesitate to offer Echon evidence of his prowess.¹⁰

First of all, the shaman said that he had never been sick. Then he described his supernatural lineage. "I am a demon," he flatly stated, although in the Wendat tongue he almost certainly used the word *oki*, which translates better as "powerful spirit." According to Tonnerawanont, "I formerly lived under the ground in the house of the demons, when the fancy seized me to become a man." He and a female *oki* entered the womb of a Wendat woman and awaited their birth. But while they gestated, Tonnerawanont grew tired of the female *oki*'s presence, so he beat her to death. The Wendat woman then gave birth to the two *okis*: the female stillborn, the male alive but deformed. Fearing evil spirits, the woman "took us both, wrapped us in a beaver skin, carried us into the woods, placed us in the hollow of a tree, and abandoned us." The misshapen boy cried so loudly that a passerby found him and brought him back to the village.¹¹

When Tonnerawanont was young, other children mocked him for his handicap, so he "caused several of them to die."¹² He then decided to turn his supernatural powers toward healing rather than destruction, and thus became a shaman. Nonetheless, the residents of Wendake must have viewed him with a mixture of fear and awe. Wendats associated bodily deformities with supernatural powers; several important figures in Wendat oral lore were handicapped. Moreover, Tonnerawanont's supreme confidence in his own abilities bolstered his reputation as someone who communed with spirits in the afterlife, for good and for ill.

When Tonnerawanont arrived in Ihonatiria, he first attended to the many sick Wendats. He then sought out the Jesuits, most of whom were still ailing, and offered his services. He said to Echon, "you will give me ten glass beads, and one extra for each patient." In return, Tonnerawanont would pray to the Wendat gods, perform a curing sweat ritual, and provide healing herbs and roots. Within three days, he assured Brébeuf, the sick Frenchmen would be entirely cured. Tonnerawanont "made a very plausible speech" according to one Jesuit, which was high praise indeed, coming from a Black Robe.[13]

Brébeuf, however, was unimpressed. He responded that because there was only one god, the Great Voice, any prayers and incantations offered by Tonnerawanont must be directed to the devil. His healing rituals therefore could do no good and might well do harm. Brébeuf was interested in the roots and herbs, however, because natural remedies would not contravene his religious scruples. Tonnerawanont—apparently without payment—described how to use two roots that were particularly effective against fevers. But the Jesuits dismissed even this generous gesture: "we hardly took the trouble to observe their effects," as the Frenchmen soon began to improve.[14] From Brébeuf's perspective, the Christian god clearly triumphed in round one of this supernatural showdown.

Tonnerawanont, on the other hand, probably focused more on the rudeness of the Black Robes. He certainly was not daunted by the Jesuits' dismissal of his healing offer. As the epidemic continued to rage among the Wendats, Tonnerawanont provided a variety of remedies to stop the dying. In the middle of October he prescribed a game of lacrosse. There are few descriptions of what lacrosse meant to the Wendats, but among the closely related Iroquois, lacrosse was a spiritually powerful form of imitation combat. Perhaps Tonnerawanont hoped to appease the angry spirit world with a demonstration of Wendat physical prowess. Word spread quickly through Wendake that Tonnerawanont had decreed a lacrosse match, and young men from "all the villages" participated with great enthusiasm, attempting to score goals on an enormous field that was probably more than a quarter mile long.[15]

In December Tonnerawanont returned to Ihonatiria and prescribed a sweat. Curiously, the shaman wanted to perform the ritual in the Black Robes' longhouse. Even more remarkably, the Jesuits allowed him to do so, apparently so they could witness the healing rite and attempt to discredit it. Within the French longhouse Tonnerawanont set up a "little arbor," with four or five wooden poles bent over and connected at the top "in the shape of a circular table," and the whole thing covered with bark.[16] The shaman then put into the sweat lodge a half-dozen large red-hot stones, which generated terrific heat.

Twelve or thirteen Wendat men crammed themselves into the sweltering lodge with Tonnerawanont and covered themselves with skins and robes to stimulate the flow of purifying sweat. The shaman began to sing, followed by the others. Tonnerawanont then threw some tobacco onto the stones and addressed the spirit world. With fresh communications from the spirits, the supernatural healer now had additional rituals to prescribe to the residents: dances and feasts. The dozen men in the sweat lodge—including, most dismayingly for the Jesuits, an influential leader who had a short time earlier "publicly renounced the devil"—unanimously agreed to perform the rituals.[17]

During these months of sickness, the residents of Wendake eagerly awaited the diminutive healer's every pronouncement. When Tonnerawanont astonishingly declared that he, as an *oki*, could control the disease and in fact would stop its effects in one village, the residents there were certain that they were "out of danger." This kind of boast was too much for Brébeuf and the other Jesuits to abide. The day after the shaman's bold statement, the Jesuits vowed to say thirty Masses in order to beg the Christian god to "confound the devil in the person of this wretch." In other words, the Jesuits hoped that by performing thirty Masses—an extraordinary investment of time and energy—they could convince their god to continue the disease in the village and thereby humiliate the demonic Tonnerawanont. The Christian god would thus "obtain glory for himself from this public affliction." The Black Robes' prayers were answered: in the village many people remained sick, "several of whom died." By these deaths, Brébeuf and the others felt that they had demonstrated their god's superior power. "Heaven, as we hope, has gained thereby."[18]

Perhaps sensing that his reputation was beginning to suffer as the epidemic continued, Tonnerawanont launched an ad hominem attack: he accused the Black Robes of causing the disease. Not only that, but he also asserted that when sick Wendats began to improve, the Jesuits gave them something— a mysterious poison?—that caused them to die. Brébeuf was furious. He confronted Tonnerawanont directly, asking him to account for these explosive accusations. The shaman claimed that his words had been misrepresented by rumormongers. Whatever the actual case, the conflict between these two supernatural healers was coming to a head. Tonnerawanont predicted that the epidemic would soon end; Brébeuf prayed that it would not relent; Wendats continued to die.

By January 1637 Tonnerawanont's inability to halt the onslaught of death began to lessen his influence in Wendake. Fewer people followed his recommendations even though he himself remained unscathed by sickness. Then, trying to enter a longhouse, he slipped on ice and fell so hard that he broke his leg. It seems that the fracture caused an infection to set in, for over the next three weeks he weakened and it became clear he was going to die. He asked his companions to carry him to the village of his birth so he could die there. His dying wish was that, contrary to customary Wendat deathways, he would be buried in the earth so he could more easily return to the underworld, the land of the *okis*, from which he had come.

The death of Brébeuf's magical rival immediately improved the Jesuits' fortunes. In Ossossané the Black Robes found the atmosphere in one longhouse dramatically changed. "While the little sorcerer Tonnerawanont was there," the Jesuits recalled, "we had always been very badly received, especially upon the subject of baptism. We had been loaded with insults there." When several weeks earlier Brébeuf had tried to baptize a dying woman, the woman's father responded that they already had their own deathways, thank you very much: "We have a certain road that our souls take after death." We do not need your path: this was the clear implication. But after Tonnerawanont died, the Jesuits decided to try again. They found the woman prepared for death, already in the leggings and moccasins she would wear in the bark coffin on the burial scaffold. Yet the family no longer resisted their attempts to baptize the woman: "God had (it seems) changed their hearts."[19] They performed the ritual, and the woman soon died. The Jesuits believed they had saved a Wendat soul from eternal damnation.

With the epidemic reaching a peak of intensity, deathbed scenes played out across Wendake, but few encouraged the Jesuits as did the encounter in Ossossané. In fact, the vast majority of deathbed scenes were what the Jesuits considered "bad" deaths. The Jesuits, like all Europeans, made a clear distinction between "good" and "bad" deaths. Good deaths followed the European script outlined by the *Ars moriendi* or "art of dying" tradition. As we have seen, the dying person was expected to offer wisdom and forgiveness to those gathered at the bedside, trust in Christ, and accept the words of the priest who prayed and performed extreme unction as the person approached the moment of death. Deathbed scenes that deviated from this script were deemed bad deaths.

In the epidemic of 1636–1637, numerous Wendat men and women died in ways Brébeuf and the other Jesuits found problematic. Many individuals that Brébeuf hoped to baptize while they were dying, based on their seeming interest in Christianity, ultimately refused baptism. One woman, for example, seemed like a perfect candidate for baptism: several of her children had been baptized and she seemed happy that they had been struck with water. Moreover, the Jesuits had healed her after she had received a leg injury, and while they nursed her they instructed her as often as they could about Christianity. But this woman's death did not go as Brébeuf hoped. He "could never induce her to consent to baptism" as she lay dying. Her reason? "She desired only to go where one of her little sons was, who had died without baptism."[20] This proved quite a stumbling block for Brébeuf during the epidemic. Most Wendats worried that accepting baptism would mean they would be separated from their loved ones and ancestors who resided in Aataentsic's village of souls.

Brébeuf likewise frowned upon deathbed scenes that included non-Christian visions and supernatural visitations. Such interventions from the spirit world were fairly common as Wendats lay dying, but this deviated from the *Ars moriendi* script by undermining the power of the presiding priest. Such was the case when a woman had a deathbed vision that the Jesuits mocked as containing nothing but "fancies," but which nonetheless reveals Wendat ideas about the permeability of the boundary between this world and the next.

A woman was dying but refused to be baptized. The presiding Jesuit tried to scare her with descriptions of the hell that awaited her if she continued in her obstinacy, but to no avail. She cheekily replied that "she did not mind going to hell and being burned there forever." Soon she was, by all appearances, dead. But then she awoke with news from the other side. "I was dead," she calmly stated, "and had already passed through the cemetery to go directly to the village of souls, when I came upon one of my dead relatives." The deceased relation urged her to return to her village. Who else would prepare food to place in graves for souls to take to the afterlife? The woman took her relative's advice and returned to her village, resolving to live. The Jesuits ridiculed this, but their derision did not blind them to the realization that such occurrences "serve as a foundation and support for the belief they have regarding the state of souls after death."[21] The vision fits with Wendat ideas about deathbed scenes, in particular that the soul of the dying person frequently communicated with the spirit world.

The frequency of "bad" deaths such as these reflected Brébeuf's difficulties in convincing many Wendats that Christianity was the answer to their problems, even as the epidemic continued unabated in the early months of 1637. Instead, most Wendats turned to traditional strategies for dealing with sickness and death. Now that Tonnerawanont was dead, other shamans stepped forward to fill his moccasins. One of the most powerful was a blind healer named Tsondacouané. He gained his knowledge about what remedies to prescribe by embarking on a vision quest. He fasted for seven days to induce visions, consuming nothing but a little tepid water. After a few days, spirits began to appear to him, and on the sixth day they began to speak to him: "Tsondacouané, we come here to associate you with us; we are demons [*okis*], it is we who have ruined the country through the contagion." The *okis* then listed the specific spirits that had caused the disease, including one "who feeds upon the corpses of those who are drowned in the great lake, and excites storms and tempests."[22]

The *okis* told Tsondacouané what the Wendats had to do to appease the angry spirits. They must hold feasts and dances, sing songs, and sacrifice dogs. They must prepare "clear soup with strawberries." This might have seemed like a cruel joke, as it was January, but for the precious supply of dried strawberries that most families hoarded through the winter. To protect themselves from the mysterious disease, people ate as many dried strawberries as they could get their hands on. Finally, Tsondacouané urged the people of Wendake to prepare large masks made of wood and straw and hang them inside and outside their longhouses in order to frighten away the *okis* causing the sickness. Within forty-eight hours of this decree all the longhouses in several villages were covered with frightening masks. One man went so far as to place a half-dozen or so of these masks on the hearth within his longhouse. Another urged Brébeuf to protect the French longhouse with such images. Brébeuf scornfully replied that the man should place his faith in a cross rather than masks: "we already had [a cross] before our door," and "we would raise another over our cabin."[23] The man's response is not recorded, but perhaps he thought, "Well then, you cure us."

Dances and feasts and masks were traditional Wendat responses to disease, but other remedies the healers prescribed may have been influenced by Catholic deathways. Tehorenhaegnon, the powerful shaman who had locked horns with Brébeuf in 1628 over the red painted cross in front of the Jesuits' residence, performed a dramatic ceremony for the sick. Using a turkey wing, he solemnly fanned those suffering from the disease. Then a leading elder carried a "kettle filled with a mysterious water" with which Tehorenhaegnon "sprinkled the sick."[24] There is no evidence that such sprinkling was part of traditional Wendat healing practices. It is possible that Tehorenhaegnon performed this ritual, which resonated with Catholic baptism, in conscious or unconscious imitation of the Jesuits.

Other innovative practices followed. Later that winter Tsondacouané decreed that Wendat deathways needed to be reformed in light of all the dying. The blind shaman made two demands, warning that if his orders were not obeyed, the sickness would last until July. First, the people of Wendake must give the dead "no more mats, at least no new ones." Ordinarily the recently dead lay on a reed mat for three days while the deceased's family prepared a funeral. Tsondacouané did not explain why corpses should no longer lie on new mats, but clearly he hoped that a change in deathways would help end the dying.

This was likewise the rationale behind his other prescription, that the residents of Wendake "should henceforth put the dead in the ground, and that in the spring they should take them out to place them in bark tombs raised upon four posts, as usual."[25] This seems to have been a nearly unprecedented departure from standard practices. Wendats traditionally performed earth inhumation only for those who drowned or froze to death, as such bad deaths indicated the sky spirit's anger. Perhaps Tsondacouané was again influenced by Catholic deathways—in this case earth inhumation—in demanding that corpses be buried in the earth for several months before being placed on scaffolds.

The residents of Wendake may have given credit to Tsondacouané and Tehorenhaegnon for helping to end the epidemic, because in the late spring of 1637 the disease finally eased its grip on Wendake. But it was too late for Ihonatiria, which had suffered so many deaths that residents abandoned the village. The Jesuits had a longhouse built for them in Ossossané and moved their mission operations there. Everywhere in Wendake life began to return to normal. But no sooner had people taken up their familiar summer tasks than another epidemic decimated the region. The summer and fall of 1637 witnessed a new sickness, one that killed with extraordinary rapidity, some-times in less than two days from the onset of symptoms. Another 5 to 10 percent of Wendake's residents died from this disease, so in the short span between 1634 and 1637 three separate epidemics reduced the region's population by roughly 20 percent. Every family was touched by death in these grim years. During this third epidemic, however, the Jesuits remained unscathed, and so the Wendats quickly came to suspect that the Black Robes had caused the disease.

The Wendats blamed a number of things associated with the French for the sickness. In June Tsondacouané prohibited the consumption of "French snow," the Wendat term for sugar. Later that summer, people began to blame French kettles for spreading the sickness, and some vowed not to use them anymore. Others claimed that the spirit of a French woman was "infecting the whole country with her breath and her exhalations." They thought that this spirit might be the sister of Etienne Brûlé, the French trader killed in the 1620s, returned to avenge his death. Still others believed that the Jesuit images of saints—brought to Wendake to depict the holy men and women whose bones Catholics revered—were causing the disease. Wendats charged that when the Jesuits "show them [images of saints], certain tainted influ-ences issue therefrom which steal down into the chests of those who look at them."[26] This deeply troubled the Jesuits, as saints were figures of healing and compassion, and the missionaries had high hopes for using these images to demonstrate Christianity's superior healing powers.

Yet more troubling was the opinion, spread by increasing numbers of Wendats, that baptism either caused the sickness or directly killed those who were struck by water. This was a logical conclusion for the Wendats to reach because, as even the Jesuits admitted, "the greater part of those we baptize, die."[27] Fear of baptism was an enormous obstacle to the Jesuit missionary strategy, which was based on reaching a critical mass of individuals who were baptized before they died. This would greatly increase the appeal of the Chris-tian afterlife—and thus the appeal of Christian teachings—to the living. But now, when the Jesuits entered a longhouse, hoping to baptize the dying, they were turned away. Some people wrapped themselves in their fur robes and covered their faces to avoid speaking with the Jesuits. Others simply closed their doors in the Jesuits' faces.

The boldest and most aggrieved Wendats began to threaten the very lives of the Jesuits, Echon in particular, whom they considered the most powerful French shaman of all. For this reason, when the Jesuits heard reports of Brébeuf's murder—including gory details and even the name of the murderer—they believed the news without question. Soon, however, Brébeuf hastened to visit his companions and assure them that he was quite alive.

But this did not mean that Brébeuf was out of danger. In August the headmen of three of the four Wendat nations called a general assembly to determine the Jesuits' fate. The meeting began in grim fashion. The Master of the Feast of the Dead, venerated for his solemnity, stood up and described the horrors he had witnessed in the years since Brébeuf arrived in their country. Each headman then, in turn, enumerated the dead and sick in his family. They did so with extraordinary sadness in their voices. A Jesuit witness wrote, "I do not know that I have ever seen anything more lugubrious than this assembly." The elders "looked at one another like corpses, or rather like men who already feel the terrors of death."[28]

As the litany of the dead went on and on, the tone of the speakers turned from grief to indignation to rage. Remembering the seemingly endless number of deceased kin incited them, in the words of a Jesuit, "to vomit more bitterly upon us the venom which they concealed within." One man stood up and named all his relations who had been killed by the various epidemics. "Now before I follow them to the grave I must free my mind." He accused the Jesuits of deliberately spreading the infection in order to ruin Wendake. Another stood and told Brébeuf that he could save his own life only if he turned over the piece of bewitched cloth that he kept in his longhouse in order to torment the Wendats with disease. When Brébeuf denied the accusation, the man triumphantly shouted, "There! that is just the way guilty people and sorcerers talk!"[29]

Finally, the headmen allowed Brébeuf to take the floor. He rose and addressed the assembly. "I have often told you, my brothers, that we know nothing about this disease, and truly I do not think you could discover its origin—that is hidden from you. But I am going to reveal to you some infallible truths." Brébeuf then made his usual case for the glory of the Christian afterlife and the superiority of Christian deathways. The elders were not nearly as polite as Wendat social customs dictated: some showed visible signs of weariness, others even fell asleep. And when Brébeuf began to talk about the disease, the room descended into tumult as the headmen continually interrupted his speech. When it became clear that nothing could be accomplished in such a poisonous atmosphere, the meeting broke up. As Brébeuf was leaving, one man snarled, "If they split your head for you, we will not say a word."[30]

A few days after this confrontational meeting Brébeuf seems to have experienced the stress of these dangers in the form of a vivid religious vision. During evening prayers, "I thought I saw in a vision of the mind or imagination, a huge horde of demons coming toward me to devour me or at least to bite me." The demons were hideous: "those in the lead resembled horses of unusual size, and their manes were curly and long like those of goats." The vision, which lasted a couple of minutes, was "so terrifying that I have never seen anything quite like it."[31] Brébeuf probably associated these bestial demons, so eager to devour him, with the angry Wendats who continued to threaten his life.

Brébeuf's response to these threats was twofold. First, he performed the quintessentially European act of writing a will. Because he had no property to bequeath, this was more a statement of faith than a true legal will. Still, Brébeuf was careful to designate what should be done with his vestments and other material components of Catholic worship and, especially, his proudest achievement, the Wendat dictionary he had painstakingly compiled over the course of a decade. In his will Brébeuf evinced no fear of death. To the contrary, he worried that "the excess of my past wickedness . . . renders me utterly unworthy so signal a favor" as martyrdom.[32]

Brébeuf's second response drew on Wendake's cultural vocabulary. In order to communicate with the Wendats on their own terms, he held an *athataion* or farewell feast to demonstrate the "little value" that he "placed upon this miserable life." Brébeuf invited all the residents of Ossossané into the Jesuits' longhouse, and it was clear from the outset that the tone of this meeting would differ greatly from that of the previous assembly. Evidently the audience admired Brébeuf's courage in the face of death and respected his use of a traditional Wendat ritual. This time they sat in "mournful silence" as Brébeuf spoke to them "of the other life."[33] The *athataion* had its desired effect. The threats against Brébeuf and the other Jesuits finally ceased.

The question remains, why did the Wendats allow the Jesuits to stay in Wendake, even though many suspected the Black Robes of causing the diseases that killed one out of every five Wendats in three short years? They easily could have sent the Jesuits packing for Quebec. Or why did they not simply kill Brébeuf and the others? The Jesuits carried no arms and would not have defended themselves against attacks; the servants had arquebuses for hunting but were outnumbered a thousand to one by Wendat warriors. The French in Quebec were better armed but were nine hundred miles away and in no position to punish the Wendats militarily. How did the Jesuits manage to stay in Wendake despite the epidemic and threats of 1637?

The answers are complex and necessarily speculative. By the end of 1637 there were several Wendats sincerely interested in Christianity, but they represented a tiny fraction of the total population. Other Wendats feared or respected the Jesuits' magic: perhaps the Black Robes would send yet more fearsome sickness spirits if they were killed or evicted, or perhaps if they stayed their healing magic could help end the dying, the way Brébeuf's bloodletting seemed to help cure several Wendats during the 1636–1637 epidemic. But even more important was what the French alliance offered the Wendats: trade goods. French officials in Quebec had long made it clear that the Jesuit presence in Wendake was a nonnegotiable aspect of the alliance: no missionaries, no trade.

This does not mean, however, that a simple desire for the accumulation of goods—the Western-style consumption to which present-day North Americans are accustomed—induced the Wendats to maintain their alliance with the French. Kettles and knives and axes all made life easier for the Wendats, it is true, but the more powerful motivator for acquiring goods was to give them away, especially to the dead and the deceased's survivors. In a span of only a few decades, trade with Europeans had transformed the Feast of the Dead from a ritual with only a minimal material component into one where beads and kettles and beaver skins beyond counting symbolized the great Wendat reverence for the dead and their remains. Even ordinary funerals and feasts of souls now required an expensive outlay of gifts, and with the repeated epidemics, funerals were more frequent than ever. Wendats may well have feared that by breaking their alliance with the French, and by losing their source of gifts for the dead, they risked the wrath of their ancestors and the rest of the spirit world.

Shielded by this figurative armor, Brébeuf and his fellow Jesuits remained undaunted in their efforts to convert Wendats to Christianity. And finally, after a decade of efforts, they began to have some success. In 1637 Brébeuf baptized the first healthy adult convert, an influential fifty-year-old man. To mark this milestone, the Jesuits decorated the chapel within their longhouse as grandly as possible. They made a little portico covered with leaves and tinsel and displayed all the religious artifacts they had, including a dramatic image of Judgment Day, which showed what happened to the damned, "with serpents and dragons tearing out their entrails."[34] In a ceremony emphasizing how Christ died so that sinners could go to heaven, Brébeuf did not fail to remind spectators of the fate that awaited those who refused baptism.

Soon Brébeuf baptized another man, one who would become the most zealous Wendat convert to Christianity. In August thirty-five-year-old Chiwatenhwa, a member of a prominent Ossossané family, lay deathly ill in his longhouse. He had been laid low by the disease that was ripping through Wendake and feared for his life. Chiwatenhwa had been interested in Christianity ever since he witnessed Brébeuf's command performance during the April 1636 council to determine the Feast of the Dead's location. Shortly thereafter he had asked Brébeuf to strike one of his young sons with water. Now he begged Brébeuf for baptism. Echon eagerly granted his wish, bestowing upon him the Christian name of Joseph.

During his sickness Chiwatenhwa demonstrated an extraordinary deference to the Jesuits. Before taking any herbs or roots, he asked the Black Robes whether doing so contradicted Christian teachings. And he would barely make a move without their advice. One day as Chiwatenhwa's fever raged, the Jesuits covered him with skins and furs, believing the sick must never get chilled. They left to perform some tasks; Chiwatenhwa sweltered. For several hours he lay in the August heat, barely able to breathe with the furs covering his head, too scared to remove them for fear of angering the Great Voice or his earthly representatives. Finally the Jesuits returned and Chiwatenhwa meekly asked them if they might remove the covers so he could have some air. The embarrassed Jesuits quickly did so.

Within two days Chiwatenhwa recovered, and from that point his faith in Christ filled him with strength rather than weakness. This was evident when his longhouse was full of sick and dying kin. His children, his nephews and nieces, his sister-in-law with a baby at her breast—all were dangerously ill. Chiwatenhwa asked the Jesuits to strike them with water, in light of his own miraculous recovery shortly after being baptized. In some cases the ritual seemed to work; in others the ill died anyway. In those cases Chiwatenhwa took comfort from Christianity, even as his favorite child, a seven-year-old whose baptismal name was Thomas, lay dying. Chiwatenhwa did not question the Christian god's reasons for afflicting him; instead, according to the Jesuits, "he offered him [the child] a hundred times a day to God, in terms of a truly Christian confidence." He took his dying son into his arms and said, "Thomas, my dear child, we are not the masters of your life; if God wishes you to go to Heaven, we cannot keep you upon earth."[35] Indeed, the boy soon died and Chiwatenhwa asked the Jesuits to attend the funeral.

Most residents of Ossossané watched Chiwatenhwa devote himself ever more passionately to Christianity and decided that he was foolish not to use sweats and feasts to try to cure his sick family. Some mocked him and his kin, derisively calling them "the family of believers."[36] A few even claimed that he was in league with the Jesuits to try to destroy Wendake with disease. Through all this Chiwatenhwa remained firm in his belief.

Over the next several years Chiwatenhwa learned so much about Christianity that he became a lay preacher. When the Jesuits were away from Ossossané, Chiwatenhwa led prayers in the chapel. At councils he made speeches supportive of the Jesuits and Christianity. He helped the Jesuits with their continued study of the Wendat language, speaking word endings slowly and distinctly so they could finally unravel the mystery of conjugations. He learned to write and, with somewhat greater difficulty, to read in Wendat. This earned him the praise of his teachers, who deemed him a man of "superior mind." The Jesuits "wondered at" his extraordinary memory, "for he forgets nothing of what we teach him." Chiwatenhwa's ability to read and write not only rendered him valuable to the Jesuits, who called him "the pearl of our Christians," but also gave him a skill mastered by almost no other Wendats.[37] Chiwatenhwa was suddenly a very important man in Wendake: a "cultural broker," as historians put it, someone able to negotiate between two cultures.

But Chiwatenhwa embraced Christianity not only for the notoriety it gained him. His new faith also brought him comfort, strength, and certainty. Chiwatenhwa, whose parents were dead, saw the Christian god as a surrogate parent. "God alone," he told the Jesuits, "has served me as father and mother." By this he meant that the Christian god gave him companionship, through dialogues in prayer, and protection. The latter motivation can be seen even more clearly when he prayed, "all men, and even all the demons of hell, can do nothing against me." He continued, "I have on my side the angels, who are in greater number than all men, and all the saints of Paradise." The saints in heaven—men and women whose bones he revered—helped protect him against natural and supernatural enemies. Finally, Chiwatenhwa drew strength from the Christian afterlife, and particularly from believing that he stood on the right side of a stark good/evil divide. When lecturing a non-Christian Wendat, he proclaimed the simple duality of Christianity: "There is but one sole master of all the world; those who serve him will be forever happy; those who offend him and do not obey him will be burned after their death."[38] Chiwatenhwa was certain that he had made the correct choice and therefore would be rewarded after death.

Other aspects of Christianity may have resonated with the convert's earlier Wendat beliefs. Because the Jesuits trusted him so deeply, they allowed Chiwatenhwa to participate in the sacrament of Holy Communion, a ritual he found especially meaningful. As one Jesuit wrote, "it is there [to the communion table] that he repairs to enjoy devotion with an incredible delight."[39] After Chiwatenhwa consumed Christ's body and blood, he prayed fervently to the Christian god, thanking him for the privilege of so powerful a ritual. It is possible that Chiwatenhwa drew on communion's resonances with Wendat ritual cannibalism, in which consuming flesh and blood allowed one to gain the power of the individual being ingested.

Likewise, Chiwatenhwa's devotion to the bones of saints may have drawn on the Wendat reverence for human remains. In the summer of 1639 Chiwatenhwa made the long journey to Quebec with the trading convoy. He was pleased to meet the Ursuline nuns, whom he described as "holy maids dressed in black, of frail constitution." He collected several heavy bundles that the French entrusted him to bring to the Jesuits in Wendake. Tucked inside one package were the "precious relics" of saints, which excited Chiwatenhwa's imagination.[40] He had long prayed to the saints, and now he was responsible for carrying their bodily remains.

Carefully guarding his holy cargo, Chiwatenhwa set off for Wendake. Even though the bundles were extremely heavy, filled with reliquaries and other supplies, he would let no other person carry them. This meant that at each portage around rapids, Chiwatenhwa had to make three or four trips to lug the packages along the river to the next point where it was safe to put the canoe back into the river. During these exhausting portages he spoke tenderly to the saints whose relics he transported, "whom he loved and honored, inasmuch as they were friends of God." Later that summer, after he had safely reached Ossossané, he continued to speak to the relics. "Great saints, I do not know your names; nevertheless you cannot be ignorant of the fact that I have brought your relics to this country. Have pity on me; pray your master and mine, Jesus, for me."[41] Like Brébeuf, whose experience with French charnel houses prepared him to understand the Feast of the Dead, Chiwatenhwa's cultural inheritance—including a language in which the words for "bones" and "souls" were almost identical—made for a relatively easy transition to a belief in the power of holy bones.

The parallels between Christianity and Wendat religion were apparent to others and likewise helped smooth the way to accepting the Black Robes' teachings. By the summer of 1639 the Jesuits estimated that there were about one hundred sincere believers in Wendake. They attributed much of their success to the model provided by their "pearl," Chiwatenhwa, and although a hundred converts represented but a tiny fraction of the roughly sixteen thousand surviving Wendats, Brébeuf and his fellow missionaries looked forward to the time when all Wendats would serve Christ. Brébeuf's goal of a Christian Feast of the Dead seemed daily to be closer to reality.

But the increasing number of Christian converts led to mounting tensions with traditionalists, those who maintained their precontact Wendat beliefs and customs. At first traditionalists could ignore the Black Robes and their handful of converts, but by the 1640s it became clear that the threat of Christianity was not going away. Chiwatenhwa was among the first to pay the price for the escalating antagonism. On August 2, 1640, he was brutally murdered while cutting some trees. When he did not return from his errand, his family members went to look for him. They found him "stone-dead and covered with blood."[42]

The Jesuits attributed Chiwatenhwa's death to Iroquois warriors, which is not entirely implausible. The Wendats' long-standing enemies had been increasing their attacks on Wendake in an effort to gain control of the valuable fur trade, and killing Chiwatenhwa may have been meant to terrorize residents of Ossossané. But there are also signs that traditionalist Wendats killed Chiwatenhwa as a warning to those contemplating accepting Christianity. This sort of murder—on the outskirts of the village, with no witnesses, but with the body easily found—is precisely how Wendats dealt with shamans and witches suspected of practicing black magic.

Whatever the case, this was a terrible blow to the Jesuits and the small community of Christian Wendats. They honored the man Brébeuf called "our fine Christian convert" with a funeral of "great solemnity" two days after his murder.[43] But the somber beauty of a Catholic funeral could not paper over the dangers caused by the rift between traditionalist and Christian Wendats. The harmony nurtured by the Feast of the Dead was now a thing of the past.

Conversion and Conflict

ONE MANIFESTATION OF THE SPLIT between Christian and traditionalist Wendats was their competing encounters with the supernatural world. Two visions from the early 1640s illustrate what divided the two factions—and what they still shared. In 1643 Etienne Totiri, a zealous Christian convert, had a "dream" or "vision"—the Jesuits couldn't decide what to call it. Totiri narrated his supernatural experience: "I saw a cross in the sky, all red with blood, and our Lord stretched thereon, with his head to the East and his feet to the West." Totiri also saw "a crowd of people advancing from the West, whom our Lord attracted by his loving looks, and who did not dare to approach his sacred head, but remained respectfully at his feet." This visual spectacle soon included an aural component. "Remaining silent and quite astounded in the midst of that company, I heard a voice commanding me to pray. I did so, in holy awe, and felt in my soul emotions of fear and of love that surpass all my thoughts."[1] The Jesuits interpreted Totiri's crowd of adoring people to represent the Neutral Nation of Indians. The Black Robes were amazed that this vision prefigured Totiri's own missionary work later that year among the Neutrals.

A few years earlier, during an epidemic, a traditionalist experienced a very different vision. A man from the village of Contarea was fishing when a spirit appeared to him in the form of a "tall and handsome young man." The *oki* spoke to the astonished fisherman: "Fear not, I am the master of the Earth, whom you Wendats honor under the name of Iouskeha. I am the one whom the French wrongly call Jesus, but they do not know me." Iouskeha brought valuable information about the source of the disease. "It is the strangers who alone are the cause of it; they now travel two by two throughout the country, with the design of spreading the disease everywhere." The spirit's advice was simple: "drive out from your village the two Black Robes who are there."[2]

These visions obviously communicated opposing messages. One indicated that the word of Christ spread by the Jesuits would attract not only the Wendats but also other nearby Indian nations. The other showed that the Jesuits hoped to destroy Wendake and therefore must be expelled immediately. But beneath this surface polarity greater complexity lurks. In particular, Christians continued to draw on traditional Wendat categories for understanding the supernatural world. Adult converts to Christianity could not instantly throw off a lifetime of stories they had listened to, rituals they had participated in, and social norms they had absorbed. They were attracted to those aspects of Christianity—and there were many, especially regarding deathways—that resonated with traditional Wendat beliefs.

As a result, Totiri's vision contained images that had long been powerful among Wendats: blood and sky. Christ's cross was red with blood, the vital substance that Wendat healers drew from the sick by sucking on incisions and that Wendat warriors drew from their tortured enemies to mingle with their own blood. The Lord appeared in the sky, home of not only Iouskeha and Aataentsic but also the sky spirit, the omnipresent *oki* who watched a person's every move. Even the simple fact that Totiri credited his "dream" or "vision" with predictive powers drew on Wendat traditions of dream interpretation.

Thus, Christian and traditionalist Wendats shared much as they interpreted the events of the early 1640s. But this did not lessen the tensions between them. The two factions focused on the differences that separated them rather than the similarities that united them. Both believed there was too much at stake in this supernatural competition to do otherwise.

At the end of the 1630s the Jesuit mission underwent several important changes that shaped events in the 1640s. In August 1638 Brébeuf stepped down as the mission's Father Superior. This was not a demotion; from the start the position had been a short-term one. The Jesuits felt that rotating the role of Superior prevented burnout. For his part, Brébeuf stated that he was happy to be relieved of the administrative burdens. He settled in as a missionary in the Cord-Making Nation.

Replacing Brébeuf as Superior was Jérôme Lalemant. Recently arrived from France, Lalemant was renowned for his administrative abilities. But he had no familiarity with the Wendats—or any other missionary experience for that matter. He came to Wendake with big plans for change, based more on Jesuit experiences elsewhere than the specific conditions among the Wendats. Lalemant had been impressed by reports of Jesuit success in Paraguay, South America. Jesuits working among the Guaraní Indians had built centralized mission centers quite different from Wendake's village-based mission. In Paraguay the Jesuits were able to persuade many Guaranís to leave their villages and move to the mission centers, where they learned about Christianity and labored for the priests. Over 140,000 Guaranís eventually moved to the centralized missions, where they (not incidentally) generated handsome profits for the Jesuits through their production of export commodities such as yerba maté tea, tobacco, and animal hides.

With Paraguay in mind, Lalemant's first order of business was to construct a centralized mission complex in Wendake. In 1639 work began on the palisaded village that would come to be known as Sainte-Marie among the Hurons. The site would eventually grow to eight hundred feet long by two hundred feet wide and contain numerous buildings, including European-style dwellings, a chapel for the Jesuits and the French workmen, longhouses for Christian and non-Christian Indian visitors, and the Indian church of St. Joseph, deliberately built with the high ceilings and overall dimensions of a longhouse. The French were pleased to have some buildings in Wendake that looked like home, and they were also excited about Sainte-Marie's chickens, pigs, and cows, which allowed for the production of the longed-for foods of France: meat, milk, cheese, and eggs.

Within a few years the French population of Sainte-Marie reached fifty-eight, including the Jesuits, workers, and servants, which represented one-fourth of the Europeans in New France. But the mission never fulfilled Lalemant's dream of a mission center surrounded by Wendat longhouses. Ties of village and family were too strong to abandon, even for Christian Wendats.

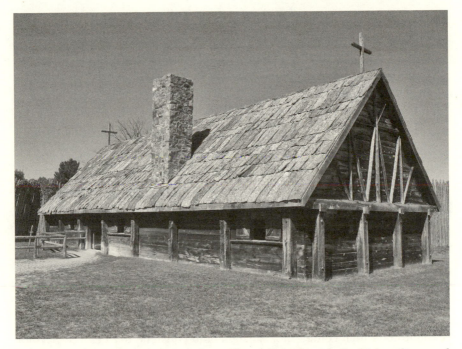

Reconstructed Church of St. Joseph. Deliberately built with the high ceilings and overall dimensions of a longhouse, the Church of St. Joseph became increasingly busy as Iroquois attacks intensified during the 1640s. This reconstruction is based on the archaeological work of Wilfrid Jury in 1950 and must be considered only a best guess about the materials the French used to build the church. Photograph by the author.

But Sainte-Marie did become an important place for converts to visit. Many walked several miles weekly to attend Sunday services there, on the day of the week that the Jesuits translated as "the true day" in Wendat.[3] Others used the site as a hostel of sorts as they traveled through Wendake to hunt or fish or trade, stopping in for food and shelter and receiving a lesson in Christian teachings.

Still other Christian Wendats hoped to die there, which gave the Jesuits an opportunity to preside over some deaths they considered "good." Because the Jesuit descriptions of "good" deaths drew so much from the European *Ars moriendi* literature, these sources must be used carefully. Missionaries may have squeezed their narratives of model Wendat deaths into preexisting story lines, thereby obscuring the details of what actually happened on the deathbeds. These are some of the accounts they left.

According to the Jesuits, a Christian woman from Ossossané, five months pregnant and in fine health, went to visit kin some thirty miles from her village. While staying with her relatives, she took ill. At first the sickness did not seem life-threatening, but nonetheless she surprised her family by telling them she needed to head to Sainte-Marie. "I leave you," she reportedly said, "because I wish to die among the faithful, and near my brothers who bring the words of eternal life. They will assist me at death, and I desire that they attend to my burial." Her wish was not merely for the Jesuits to care for her on earth. "I shall rise again with them, and I do not wish my bones to be mingled with those of my deceased relatives, who will be nothing to me in eternity."[4] This was a dramatic renunciation of traditional Wendat beliefs. According to the Jesuits, the pregnant woman preferred the solitary grave of a Christian burial to the communal ossuary of the Feast of the Dead.

So she got into a canoe, paddled back to Ossossané, and then walked nine miles to Sainte-Marie. Once inside the compound's "hospital" or infirmary, her condition deteriorated. She experienced a long and painful illness, always resigned to God's will, before it was clear she was going to die. The Jesuits brought her a final communion so she could consume her beloved Savior's body and blood one last time. Just before she died she gave birth to a tiny premature boy, who lived just long enough to be baptized. Moments later the woman likewise died. The Jesuits now realized they needed to consecrate a cemetery, which they did right next to the Indian church of St. Joseph. After a "solemn" funeral, this woman became the first person buried in the cemetery.[5] Her family would not caress her bones in preparation for a Feast of the Dead.

This cemetery became a beacon for the Christians of Wendake. Some who died in their villages wished to be brought there, even though most villages with even modest Christian contingents now had small consecrated burial grounds. Christine Tsorihia was one such woman. She had been baptized several years before contracting her mortal illness and had long been devoted to the Virgin Mary. As she lay dying, she had a dramatic vision. "O my son," she reportedly asked, "do you not see the rare beauty of that great lady, all brilliant with light, who stands at my side?" Her son, also a Christian, responded, "My mother, you are dreaming. I see nothing, and how can you say you do, since your eyes are closed?" Enraptured, Tsorihia said, "Oh, how beautiful it is to see her," and then died.[6] Her family carried her corpse the twenty miles to Sainte-Marie to fulfill her wish to be buried there. She was the second to be interred in the cemetery—and yet another Wendat who would not be part of the Feast of the Dead.

From the Jesuits' perspective these were good deaths and burials, following the script to the letter. But the material record at Sainte-Marie paints a more complex picture of the burials. In the late 1940s archaeologists at the mission unearthed twenty-one graves holding roughly twenty-five individuals (some graves appeared to contain multiple children). It is not surprising that seven Christian Wendats were buried with rosaries, the beads European Catholics used as a counting device to help them keep track of their prayers. The presence of rosaries in these Christian Wendat graves fits comfortably with contemporary French practice: burial with rosaries became widespread after the mid-sixteenth-century Council of Trent inspired efforts to educate the laity using prayer beads.

But almost all the graves also contained evidence of traditional Wendat practices. The Jesuits left no record of these Wendat burial customs at Sainte-Marie. It is unclear whether this represents Jesuit ignorance, lack of interest, or a desire to cover up non-Christian practices. Whatever the case, the burials at Sainte-Marie offer clear evidence of syncretism, the blending of religious traditions and other cultural practices. All of the individuals were buried in wooden coffins according to the European style. Some of the deceased were placed into the coffins on their back, as Europeans were, while others were buried in a flexed position, on the side with the knees pulled up to the chest, just as in a Wendat scaffold burial. Some of the burials were oriented east-west, as in Europe, others north-south.

Even more striking are the grave goods other than rosaries that were included with almost every burial. The Jesuits derided such items as being useless to the deceased, but this apparently did not faze those who prepared the corpses for interment. One woman was buried with a small cache of shell beads by her side; another person was placed into the coffin with about a pint of basswood seeds. Others had in their graves pipe stems and potsherds. One grave contained the teeth and jawbone of a dog.

The most dramatic burial was the one archaeologists labeled Grave 19. Two skeletons were squeezed inside one coffin. A man lay on his side with his knees flexed; with him was a smaller skeleton, probably a woman, disarticulated and deposited like a burial bundle for the Feast of the Dead. Accompanying these two bodies were several rare and costly European metal items. The coffin held a small copper pot, five inches in diameter, an iron knife, and an extraordinary fourteen-inch-long pewter pipe with fleurs-de-lis carved on its bowl. Archaeologists speculated that the intact skeleton was a high-status Wendat man and the bundle burial was his wife. The woman, according to this theory, died before her husband and had been buried on a scaffold in traditional Wendat fashion. Later, the man became a Christian, and when he died his wife's skeleton was removed from the scaffold, cleaned and bundled, and placed within his coffin.

Whether or not that is Grave 19's backstory, this cemetery, with its flexed burials and shell beads and dog teeth, offers yet more evidence that adult converts—even those so zealous that they begged to be buried at Sainte-Marie—drew heavily on traditional Wendat customs. These converts were especially attracted to aspects of Christianity that resonated with their earlier beliefs. Burial with rosaries, for example, made perfect sense to people who had long adorned the dead with shell beads. Even though tensions between Wendat factions remained high, Christians were closer to traditionalists in many of their fundamental assumptions than either group realized.

The struggle between the two factions over how to define proper burial practices remained crucial because so many Wendats continued to die from European diseases. From the autumn of 1639 to the spring of 1640 the worst epidemic to date ravaged Wendake. This time the killer was smallpox, the European disease most feared by the indigenous peoples of the Americas because of its horrifying symptoms and devastatingly high mortality rate. A person infected with the smallpox virus first developed symptoms similar to a very bad case of the flu: high fever, vomiting, and intense pain in the back and stomach. Then the symptoms eased and the person might think she had escaped alive. But soon the characteristic smallpox pustules developed, first in the mouth and throat, and then, even more painfully, on the soles of the feet, palms, and face. If the pustules ran together in a stinking, suppurating mass, the prognosis was not good. At least 60 percent of such individuals with "confluent" smallpox died, usually after ten days to two weeks of suffering.

Because almost all Europeans were exposed to the smallpox virus as children and thus developed lifetime immunity, the French did not succumb to this horrible disease. Not a single Frenchman took ill. By contrast, nearly half of all Wendats died in this epidemic; many others bore the telltale scars for life. By the time smallpox finished tormenting the Wendats, their population was down to nine thousand, a decrease of roughly 60 percent in less than a decade.

This extraordinary level of mortality caused the Wendats no end of grief. According to the Jesuits, "the death of their nearest relatives takes away their reason." With almost everyone in a state of mourning, the Wendats' anger and confusion began to mount. Baptized Wendats started to doubt that the Christian god was as benevolent as advertised. After the death of one especially zealous Christian, "it was everywhere said that God was forsaking his most faithful servants, [and] that the Faith availed only to cause them to die." According to the Jesuits, the Wendats believed "that our desire to put them in Heaven as soon as possible caused us to hasten the days of those whom we believe to be the best prepared therefor."[7]

Thus, the widespread deaths, combined with French resistance to the scourge, caused the Wendats—traditionalists and even many Christians— once again to blame the Jesuits for the disease. They singled out Brébeuf in their accusations. Some claimed that when Echon first entered Wendake he had said, "I shall be here so many years, during which I shall cause many to die, and then I shall go elsewhere to do the same, until I have ruined the whole land." Others alleged that during Chiwatenhwa's funeral Brébeuf turned in the direction of the Senecas, the Iroquois nation that the Black Robe blamed for Chiwatenhwa's murder, and intoned, "Senecas, it is all over with you; you are dead."[8] Smallpox now raged among the Senecas, proving Brébeuf's power as a sorcerer. As in 1637, these rumors fueled threats against Brébeuf's life. The situation became so dangerous that Lalemant ordered his most experienced missionary to return to Quebec. In May 1641, having been away from Quebec for seven years, Brébeuf wedged his large body into a canoe and paddled away from Wendake.

If this delighted traditionalist Wendats, their pleasure was short-lived, because Wendake soon faced another, potentially more devastating threat: Iroquois attacks. The destruction of a Wendat village in 1642 by Iroquois warriors signaled a new phase in the decades-long rivalry between the two groups. Since at least 1600, Mohawks, the easternmost nation of the Iroquois, had been eager to acquire European goods. Like the Wendats, the Mohawks coveted European trade items not only because they promised comfort and convenience but also because the goods abounded with spiritual power. Mohawks (and members of other Iroquois nations) buried many of their newly acquired European items with the dead.

To obtain these powerful goods, the Mohawks needed to look north, toward the St. Lawrence River, where they could trade for French hatchets and kettles. This, however, put them in conflict with several Algonquian groups that controlled the St. Lawrence. Thus, the Mohawks were pleased when Dutch traders arrived on the Hudson River in the 1610s and when the colony of New Netherland established Fort Orange (later Albany) just to the east of Mohawk territory in 1624. Now the Mohawks had easy access to European goods—and they didn't have to deal with a Dutch version of the Jesuits. For Dutch Protestants in New Netherland, missionary work was a much lower priority than for French Catholics in Quebec.

In exchange for furs the Mohawks received metal items such as nails and knives from the Dutch. They also traded for a great deal of cloth; the Mohawks called the Dutch not only "ironworkers," a parallel to the Wendat "iron people" moniker for the French, but also "cloth makers." Much more so than Wendats, Mohawks supplemented their traditional wardrobe of skins and furs with European wool and cotton. From an early stage in their relationship with the Dutch, the Mohawks evinced a strong desire for European goods.

Guns were among the most coveted items. As a Dutch author wrote, the Mohawks "are exceedingly fond of guns, sparing no expense for them."[9] The Mohawks had been introduced to the terrifying power of firearms in their 1609 defeat at the hands of Champlain and his new Wendat allies. In reality, guns were not as great a technological advantage over bows and arrows as they might seem in retrospect. The firearms of the early seventeenth century—called arquebuses by the French and matchlocks by the English—earned their English name because one needed to apply a lighted fuse to the powder in order to make it fire. (These would later be replaced by flintlocks, which used flint to spark the powder.) Matchlocks were extremely heavy, slow to load, and difficult to use in the rain. An experienced bowman could fire five or six arrows in the time it took to reload a matchlock. But guns had a potent psychological effect, as the Mohawks had discovered in 1609. After their headmen had been slain by Champlain's roaring weapon, Mohawk resistance disintegrated in fear and confusion.

Through the 1630s, however, Mohawks were able to obtain only a limited number of guns. The Dutch West India Company, which had a monopoly on the fur trade at Fort Orange, followed the practice of the French at Quebec and banned the sale of guns to native people, fearing that Indian access to firearms might enable the destruction of their small European outposts. This policy changed in 1639 when the Dutch West India Company lost its monopoly over the fur trade. Now individual colonists were free to do business with

Indians, and they quickly found that guns were the most profitable item they could trade for furs. Realizing that the Iroquois acquisition of firearms imperiled Wendake, the French reluctantly began to trade guns with the Wendats, but only in very limited quantities, and only with Christians, whose numbers remained small. Through the 1640s the Wendats had far fewer firearms than their Iroquois enemies.

From the Mohawk perspective, guns were the key to their strategy for extending Iroquois domination beyond its current boundaries. Central New York was not the best location to acquire the furs—particularly beaver—that the Dutch so dearly desired. Not only was Iroquoia's fur-bearing population relatively small, but the pelts were not nearly as thick as those farther north. As a result, in the 1630s Mohawks began to attack Wendat trading convoys on their way to Quebec, canoes laden with furs. Even this did not sate the Mohawk appetite for pelts, so in the early 1640s they joined forces with another Iroquois nation, the powerful Senecas. Residents of this westernmost Iroquois nation, the one closest to Wendake, traded with the Mohawks for firearms to prepare for an assault on the Wendats. Now well armed, the Senecas and Mohawks attacked Wendake itself, hoping to find inside longhouses yet more pelts awaiting the journey to Quebec.

But a desire for furs was not the only motivation for Iroquois attacks on Wendake. At least as important was the Iroquois practice of "mourning war": taking captives to replace individuals killed by warfare or disease. Although Wendats also adopted captives, the Iroquois naturalized far more outsiders into their nations. In the wake of several epidemics, the forcible adoption of outsiders became the cornerstone of Iroquois foreign policy. Starting in 1633, European diseases similar to those in Wendake ravaged the Iroquois. By the early 1640s the Mohawk population had declined by perhaps 75 percent; other Iroquois nations were only marginally better off. As a result, the Iroquois undertook mourning wars to provide captives who would replace the deceased.

Wendake was the primary target for Iroquois mourning wars. The Iroquois knew that the Wendats spoke a closely related language, held similar religious beliefs, lived in nearly identical longhouses, and ate many of the same foods. No group could be assimilated as easily as the Wendats, the Iroquois believed. As a Jesuit captive in Iroquoia explained, "The design of the Iroquois, as far as I can see, is to take, if they can, all the Hurons; and, having put to death the most considerable ones and a good part of the others, to make of them both but one people and only one land."[10] So when the Senecas and Mohawks attacked Wendake looking for furs, they just as eagerly sought prisoners to bring back to their homelands.

Thus it was that in June 1642 Iroquois warriors rudely awakened residents of a small village in eastern Wendake by setting fire to the longhouses. The surprise attack left the village in ashes. The Iroquois killed or took captive nearly every man, woman, and child. Only twenty or so Wendats escaped the flames and arrows and made their way to a neighboring village with the terrifying news. The Iroquois threat, which had seemed distant when it was confined to the St. Lawrence, had come to Wendake.

Wendats, however, were unable to mount a unified resistance. Christians and traditionalists agreed they must attack the Iroquois, but they could not see eye to eye on the details. Traditionalists prepared for battle by consulting a renowned shaman. The supernatural seer ordered a sweat lodge erected, where, amid the red-hot stones, he communicated with an *oki*. The spirit brought good news. "Victory! Victory!" the shaman cried, "I see the enemies coming toward us from the south. I see them take to flight. I see all of you, my comrades, making prisoners of them."[11] Full of martial passion, the traditionalists headed south, sure of their impending triumph over the Iroquois.

The Christians hesitated. Should they follow the advice of a spirit they now considered a "demon"? One young man resolutely addressed the Christian god. "If the promises of the demon are fulfilled, he alone will derive glory therefrom, and your name will be blasphemed for it." This man urged his fellow Christians to follow a different strategy. "Let us rather go toward the west, from where our enemies most frequently come."[12] Thus divided, the Wendats headed in different directions to confront the Iroquois. As it happened, the traditionalists had chosen the correct direction, but they suffered a stinging defeat. They killed not a single Iroquois, lost several of their own men, and then retreated from the field of battle.

This episode demonstrates the growing self-confidence of Wendake's Christians. As their numbers slowly increased in the early 1640s, they more firmly declared which aspects of Christianity attracted them. More often than not these revolved around deathways, and the Christian afterlife in particular. In Ossossané there lived a "poor little man" named Matthias Atiessa who was the "butt of the village" for his lack of wit. Dressed in ragged skins, he cut a most unimpressive figure, yet he had the audacity to dispute a village leader's characterization of Christianity. The headman, turning Jesuit terminology on its head, argued that Christianity consisted of nothing but "diabolical remedies and dances." He asked Atiessa, "what do the Black Robes give you, to induce you to believe?" "Paradise" was the man's simple reply.[13] For him, heaven was Christianity's greatest lure, a place more comfortable than even the Wendats' pleasant village of souls.

Likewise, a woman of the Cord-Making Nation was especially attracted to the doctrine of the resurrection, which asserts that on Judgment Day bodies will rise from the grave and be reunited with their souls. One day the Jesuits preached a sermon on resurrection, which touched her deeply. She called out to the assembled audience, "This it is that makes us believe." If traditionalists kill us, she said, so be it. "I shall rise again some day, in the body that they shall have killed."[14] This doctrine made sense to many Wendats in part because of their traditional belief that souls could be reanimated in new bodies. Accepting this Christian principle required only a modest modification of earlier beliefs.

Conversely, fear of hell was also a powerful motivator for conversion. With this belief, however, there was no parallel in the traditional Wendat belief system. An old Christian man in Ossossané, for example, burned with fever. He tossed and turned and could get no rest. When he finally recovered, he thanked the Christian god for healing him, but he also remembered the fever with which he had burned and decided to use this experience as a lesson. So he burned himself with an actual fire. A friend urged him to remove himself from the flames. "No, no," the man responded, "thus do I learn that it is a bad thing to offend God, unless we are resolved to burn in a fire from which we can never withdraw, and of which this one is but a shadow." There was no Wendat analogue to the Christian hell; instead, this man drew on Wendat traditions of stoicism and self-searing. As Gabriel Sagard had written in a discussion of Wendat healing, "I wondered also to see them burn themselves on their bare arms with the pith of the elder-tree for the pleasure of it, letting it burn away and smolder on them, in such wise that the wounds, scars, and cicatrices [scar tissue] remained there indelibly."[15] This man displayed a similar pleasure in pain, yet for the different end of reinforcing his Christian belief.

At this point in the early 1640s, with more than a hundred baptized adults and several hundred others actively learning from the Black Robes, the Christian community began to reach that critical mass for which the Jesuits had so long hoped. In the early years of the mission, the Wendat love for their children and other relatives had worked against the adoption of Christianity. The

Christian afterlife had been a major obstacle for many individuals because they shuddered to think that they might spend eternity separated from their loved ones who had already gone to Aataentsic's village of souls. But as more and more Wendats were baptized, and as many of those died, this began to attract their relatives who wished to follow them to the Christian afterlife.

The memory of the zealous convert Joseph Chiwatenhwa thus proved a powerful lure for the rest of his family. When his three-year-old daughter lay dying, she "frequently pointed to heaven saying that she was looking for her father, and wished to go with him." When this girl was buried in Ossossané's Christian cemetery, some of her baptized relatives paused to weep at Chiwa-tenhwa's grave. His widow, Marie Aonetta, chastised them: "What is the good of all these tears? Let us endeavor to follow them up there, in heaven; let us gather there an entire family of saints." Another man, a devoted Christian, urged his friends to become Christians, "so that," he said, "we shall all go to heaven in company."[16] The strength of Wendat social and familial ties began to have a multiplier effect on baptisms: new converts exerted a strong influence over their friends and family members who hoped to spend eternity together.

Many of these converts made a decisive break with traditional Wendat burial customs. One elderly Christian man, perhaps seventy years old, had a stroke and lost use of an arm. Traditionalists mocked his faith, saying that the Christian god surely had no love for this newly crippled man. He responded that the deterioration of his body did not bother him, as he expected that "one day I shall rise again in glory." He asserted that "this dying body must rot in the ground before it can become immortal."[17] A traditional Wendat scaffold burial, he believed, would not allow him to experience the resurrection he desired.

Even more surprising was that some Christian Wendats began to renounce the Feast of the Dead. On Easter Sunday 1642, a group of Christians prepared for war against the Iroquois. Because they hailed from several Wendat nations, they decided to hold a council in order to avoid any miscommunication about their goals. They agreed that they would lodge only with other Christians and that they would not gossip about one another with any traditionalists. Given that they were likely to die, they specified their new beliefs about burial: "Let us inform our relatives who are not of the same faith as we, even if they be our fathers and our children, that we do not wish our bones to be mingled together after our death, since our souls will be eternally separated." A Jesuit witness to this oath was surprised because "if there be anything in the world that is sacred among the Hurons, it is their law of burial."[18] In 1636

Brébeuf had hoped for a Christian Feast of the Dead. Now, just six years later, it seemed to the Jesuits that the Wendats would perhaps not even need that hybrid ritual to attract them to Christianity. Christian burial—single earth interments in consecrated cemeteries—might soon replace the Feast of the Dead.

Ironically, this development occurred just as the Feast was expanding its geographical range. Long confined to Wendake, the Feast of the Dead spread among neighboring Algonquian peoples who had attended the Wendat ritual. They had evidently been impressed by the ritual's ability to symbolize harmony within and between communities and by the lavish material devotion to the deceased. In September 1642 Jesuits attended a Feast of the Dead hosted by the Nipissings some sixty miles north of Wendake. Two thousand indigenous people from as far west as Michigan participated in a ritual that drew heavily on Wendat precedent but also included unique Algonquian elements. Each nation arrived by canoe and displayed its presents: items of native manufacture such as beaver robes as well as valuable European goods such as copper kettles and iron hatchets. Dancing followed: a "ballet" of sorts that the Jesuits found a "pleasure" to watch, accompanied by "harmonious" music.[19] The Black Robes were as impressed by this Feast as they were by the Wendat version.

Women played a leading role in the Algonquian Feast. They were among the chief dancers, and they helped build an enormous structure—roughly a hundred yards long—where the Feast itself took place. Women carried the bones of the dead into this "magnificent room." The bones were nestled in fresh beaver skins and decorated with wampum necklaces. Men and women then sang a "sweet and sad" song to demonstrate their grief.[20] There is no description of what ultimately happened to the bones, but they were likely buried in a communal ossuary in the Wendat fashion. Indeed, some Wendats attended and may have offered advice about the ritual. For the rest of the seventeenth century, Algonquian peoples from east of Lake Huron to the Straits of Mackinac held Feasts of the Dead. The ritual seems to have died out among Algonquians in the early eighteenth century under pressure from French missionaries.

Back in Wendake, traditionalists did their best to counter the increasing self-confidence of Christians. Traditionalists hoped to keep alive the customs—including the Feast of the Dead—that nourished their sense of connection between the past and the present, between ancestors and offspring.

But first they had to fend off another round of Iroquois attacks. Iroquois warriors rocked Wendake with numerous incursions in the summer of 1643. The Iroquois reportedly possessed three hundred guns "and use them with skill and boldness."[21] Nearly every day warriors killed Wendat women working in their fields. And the Iroquois took hundreds of Wendats captive as part of their continued mourning war.

Against this terrifying backdrop, traditionalists decided that it was crucial to combat Christianity, which threatened to divide and weaken Wendake at the worst possible moment. No longer content with the characteristic Wendat "live and let live" philosophy, traditionalists did their best to make life unpleasant for converts. They disrupted Christians while they were praying, mocking them by calling them "Marians" in reference to their repeated invocation of the Virgin Mary. They ridiculed Christians as cowards, saying that they had converted only because they feared the fires of hell. And they spread rumors about the Christians, alleging that their rosaries and religious medals "caused both soul and blood to pour forth from those who looked at them in a certain manner."[22] Once again blood, central to both religions, animated the religious competition between the two factions.

Other traditionalists proved willing to cut family ties to help stem the tide of Christianity. One convert was kicked out of his longhouse by traditionalist relatives who "could not bear his observance of Christian duties." Another left home after his family urged him to renounce Christianity. When he would not do so, they no longer gave him anything to eat. A third, Etienne Totiri, found himself opposed not only by his family but also by other members of his community. Totiri, whose vision of a blood-covered cross so impressed the Jesuits, constructed a small chapel in his longhouse from boards and bark so he could pray in peace. Instead, the little structure brought him nothing but scorn after the Jesuits performed Mass in his chapel. "This," the traditionalists said, "will be the misfortune of the country." The "nearest relatives" of Totiri and his fellow Christians told them "that they must go and dwell elsewhere, or abandon the Faith, if they had any desire to live." A headman warned one Christian, "We will tear you out of the earth as a poisonous root."[23] This was the way Wendats threatened suspected sorcerers. As Chiwatenhwa's murder showed, this was not an idle threat.

Totiri had a central role in another revealing confrontation over deathways. Jesuits wanted to place an enormous cross in his village's Christian cemetery to make the burial ground more impressive. Simply erecting the cross would not make enough of a statement; rather, the Black Robes opted to carry the great cross in a procession through the whole village, from Totiri's chapel to the cemetery. The traditionalists who watched the procession mocked the Christians for paying such respect to a "trunk of wood." After the cross had been planted in the cemetery, some traditionalist children threw "stones and filth" at the cross, "which somewhat injured it."[24]

This was too much for Totiri to bear. That evening he climbed to the top of his longhouse and, with an "astounding voice," shouted the warning used when Iroquois warriors approached. Everyone came running, wondering from which direction the attack was coming. Instead, they were met with a speech by Totiri that used customary Wendat beliefs against the traditionalists. "Tremble, my brothers," he cried, "the cemetery of the Christians is profaned. God will avenge this insolence." He said that if the traditionalists did not prevent their children from desecrating the cemetery, then it was as if they had done so themselves. And as all Wendats knew, cemetery desecration was one of the most serious transgressions of social norms. "Dead bodies are sacred things," Totiri continued, "and even among you infidels they are shown respect, and one commits a crime if he touches a paddle suspended to a sepulchre."[25] In other words, just touching a gift attached to a traditional burial scaffold was offensive; deliberately desecrating a cemetery was even more so. The traditionalists could not disagree. They chastised their children, in effect admitting that Totiri was right.

But traditionalists were less willing to cede ground to those whose actions seemed to threaten the very health of the community. A woman named Luce Andotraaon discovered this to her dismay. Before her baptism she had been among a very small number of initiates in a healing society whose members performed special dances to cure the sick. The dance in which Andotraaon specialized was the "most celebrated in the country" because of its ability to harness the power of *okis* for healing. After she became a Christian, however, she no longer was willing to participate in the ritual, arguing that it went against her beliefs. Given that Wendake had lost 60 percent of its population to disease in the previous decade, the refusal of a successful healer to perform her role was too dangerous to ignore. A headman told her that he would "surprise her the next summer in her field, to split her head, and remove her scalp" unless she resumed her healing dance.[26] Andotraaon refused to be bullied and remained steadfast in her opposition to the dance. It is unclear whether the traditionalists ever made good on their threat.

As the gulf between Christians and traditionalists deepened, a divisive figure returned to Wendake. On September 7, 1644, Jean de Brébeuf stepped out of a canoe near Sainte-Marie and into a growing maelstrom. Brébeuf had spent the previous three years in Quebec, itching to return to the mission field. He had kept himself busy, running a school for native boys and young men, teaching them the finer points of Catholic doctrine. Finally, the mission Superior determined that the threats against Brébeuf's life had dissipated enough for Echon to return to Wendake. As he strode from his canoe to the mission center at Sainte-Marie, it was unclear what effect his presence would have on the Christians and traditionalists of Wendake.

seven Destruction

IN THE MID-1640S both Christian and traditionalist Wendats used supernatural visions to help them interpret the religious drama unfolding in Wendake. In this they were joined by Jean de Brébeuf, the most mystical of all the Jesuits. Brébeuf was fifty-one years old when he returned to Wendake in 1644, so one might imagine that his youthful religious zeal had cooled. Quite the contrary. As tensions rose in Wendake, Brébeuf's passionate supernaturalism only increased. He experienced a series of visions that, he believed, offered insight into the future of the Christian mission among the Wendats.

Brébeuf's mystical encounters ranged from the bizarre to the sublime. Once, while praying in preparation for Holy Communion, he had a vision of a Jesuit, but he did not know who it was. The priest was "hovering in space with only half a body and surrounded by a great light in the way they usually portray our Fathers." Soon this placid image began to change: "A little later, antennae grew out of the Jesuit's head like those we see on lobsters, then his whole head was transformed into a river crab." Brébeuf wondered if he was the Jesuit in this vision, undergoing some sort of horrible symbolic transformation, which understandably "frightened and upset" him. A more reassuring image came one day when he "seemed to see the Blessed Virgin Mary carrying the Infant Jesus on an azure blue cloud and from this cloud golden rays were bursting forth with awesome beauty."[1] Perhaps this predicted his success in Wendake, with Christ's word bursting forth over the land like rays of sunshine.

Most portentously, on October 8, 1644, just one month after arriving back in Wendake, Brébeuf experienced a blood-soaked vision. As he was praying before supper in the chapel at Sainte-Marie, this is what came to him: "I seemed to see stains of red or purple blood on the clothes of all our Fathers as well as on my own. There were no exceptions." In his spiritual journal Brébeuf tried to put a positive spin on this vision. He wrote, "the idea occurred to me that we were all covered with our righteousness as with a blood-stained garment," a likely reference to Revelation 19:13, in which the "Word of God" is "clothed with a vesture [robe] dipped in blood."[2] But there is another, more obvious reading: that the Jesuits themselves would soon be covered in blood. Whether the blood would be their own or that of the Wendats the vision did not reveal.

Starting in 1644, non-Christian Wendats began to craft a more active response to the threat of Christianity. Traditionalists had, up to this point, largely maintained continuity with their precontact rituals and beliefs. But now they deliberately adopted some new practices derived from a variety of indigenous sources in order to buttress themselves against the Christian threat. In particular, traditionalists generated opposition to Christianity through deathways. This was a new sort of resistance to the Jesuits' teachings that went beyond earlier efforts simply to ignore the Black Robes or to make life uncomfortable for new converts. Instead, this was an ideological counterattack aimed straight at the heart of what the Jesuits felt was most appealing about Christianity: its vision of a glorious afterlife for the saved.

Traditionalists asserted that they had learned from Algonquins crucial new details about the afterlife. These Algonquins had been on a long journey—they were, after all, hunter-gatherers who regularly ranged across hundreds of miles of forest and field—and had come upon "very populous cities, inhabited only by the souls which formerly had lived a life similar to ours." In these cities the souls informed the Algonquins that "things which are said of Paradise and Hell are fables." The Black Robes' teachings were nothing but lies. Traditionalist Wendats learned from their Algonquin informants that after death the soul entered a new body "more vigorous than the first" in a "more blissful country."³ This built on the long-standing Wendat belief that after the Feast of the Dead souls were sometimes reincarnated in new bodies. Traditionalists felt that the Algonquins' vision confirmed and elaborated on their beliefs.

Likewise, another vision—this one experienced by Wendats—further fueled the traditionalist counteroffensive against Christianity. Traditionalists brought reports of a giant *oki* who appeared in the woods. This figure carried Wendake's twin staffs of life: in one hand he held numerous ears of corn, in the other great quantities of fish. The *oki* said that he, not the Christian god, had created humans and taught them to plant corn, and that he had filled the lakes and seas with fish. The giant spirit also outlined an afterlife that differed from the one the Black Robes described. He said that when people died, their souls separated from their bodies and rendered deeper devotion to this giant *oki*, who in turn protected them and cared for them. The spirit finally told the Wendats that "to believe that any one of them was destined to a place of torments and to the fires" were "false notions, with which, nevertheless, we [Jesuits] strive to terrify them."⁴ Hell was an invention of the Black Robes, the spirit insisted, and therefore the Wendats had no reason to fear these false prophets.

Finally, and most dramatically, traditionalists asserted that a Christian Wendat woman had returned from the land of the dead with news that proved that the Black Robes spread falsehoods. Of all the components of the resurgent traditionalist movement, this one, according to the Jesuits, "found most credit" and became "the most powerful rhetoric of the enemies of our faith." Traditionalists said that the soul of a woman who had been buried in the Christian cemetery at Sainte-Marie had returned from the dead. Could this woman have been Tsorihia, whose dying vision of the Virgin Mary helped convince her that she wanted to be buried at Sainte-Marie? Whoever she was, she told a remarkable story.

The woman's soul left her decomposing body in its grave at Sainte-Marie and flew to the Christian heaven. The French were there, and at first they seemed to welcome the soul to its new residence. But their greeting turned into the kind of reception the Iroquois reserved for captives entering one of their villages. The woman's soul had to pass through a gauntlet in which the French burned her with firebrands and committed other "cruelties and torments." Having finally passed through this violent entrance, the woman's soul entered heaven to find that it was nothing but fire. Because it was located in the sky, the French heaven used the sun to provide the fire for their torments. The French walked around and took pleasure in burning the souls that resided there. Most perversely, the French enjoyed torturing the souls of Wendat, Algonquin, and Montagnais Christians. No traditionalists could be found in this hellish inversion of the Christian heaven. Rather, traditionalist souls went to "a place of delights, where everything good abounds, and from where all evil is banished."[5] There they danced and feasted and enjoyed fine foods.

The Christian woman's soul endured fearful tortures in the Jesuits' fiery heaven for an entire day, which felt like years. Then, as she was about to fall asleep, exhausted from her odyssey, a shadowy figure released the soul from the French heaven and showed her the way back to Wendake. The soul reentered her body and set about spreading the "terrible news" of what awaited Christians when they died.[6] She said that the only reason the Jesuits made the long journey to Wendake was to gain captives for their infernal afterlife. She urged Christian Wendats to renounce their conversions before it was too late.

"This news was soon spread everywhere," the Jesuits wrote, and "it was believed in the country without gainsaying."[7] The Christians at Ossossané said they had heard it from the Christians at Contarea, who said they had learned of it from the Christians at Scanonaenrat, and so on in an endless spiral of attribution. A revitalized traditionalist movement, with deathways at its core, began to make significant headway against the progress of Christianity in Wendake.

The Jesuits characteristically redoubled their efforts in light of this potent threat. They were in an especially good position to do so because of the leadership of their new Superior, Paul Ragueneau, who succeeded Jérôme Lalemant in 1645. Lalemant had brought impressive administrative credentials to Wendake, but his lack of experience as a missionary left him ill-prepared to understand what would best appeal to the Wendats. Sainte-Marie never lured Christian Wendats to pull up stakes and resettle there, the way Lalemant imagined it would. Ragueneau, by contrast, had spent eight years as a missionary among the Wendats and knew the language fluently.

Relying on his years of experience, Ragueneau formulated a more tolerant approach to Christianization efforts. In effect this was a return to a sixteenth-century Jesuit missionary strategy, what an Italian Jesuit referred to in 1579 as the "gentle way" to conversion. Ragueneau felt that the Jesuits in Wendake had strayed from this older strategy of overlooking "matters of indifference," local customs that did not directly contradict Catholic doctrine. He urged his fellow Jesuits to ignore minor breaches of Christian norms among the Wendats and instead to focus on the fundamental tenets of Christianity, including death-related beliefs in the afterlife and resurrection. Ragueneau insisted that "one must be very careful before condemning a thousand things among their customs." He noted that if missionaries obsessed too much about these minor details, "one thinks he is obliged to forbid as impious certain things that are done in all innocence, or, at most, are silly, but not criminal customs."[8]

To an extent this was a repudiation of Brébeuf's stricter methods as Superior in the 1630s. But Ragueneau's philosophy also reflected the changing circumstances of the mission, which now enjoyed the support of hundreds of Christian Wendats, with more baptized every year. As Ragueneau himself put it, "time is the most faithful instructor."[9] It had been more than a decade since Brébeuf and a couple of other Jesuits had founded the mission, and now Ragueneau's corps of eighteen Jesuits and hundreds of Christian Wendats gave him the luxury of adopting a more tolerant approach.

The Jesuits quickly applied Ragueneau's philosophy to how they presided over deathbed scenes. In the mid-1640s they began to tell converts that the *athataion* or farewell feast did not contradict the teachings of Christianity. This new policy shaped the deathbed scene of a six-year-old Christian boy, for example. The boy burned with fever and appeared to be dying. His mother wept, grief-stricken that her only son was mortally ill. The boy told his mother not to weep, but rather to have faith in the Christian afterlife.

Soon the boy was so close to death that he asked his mother to carry him to Sainte-Marie, so he could be buried in the Christian cemetery there. His mother agreed, but not before calling the village together for the boy's *athataion*. The Christian boy, thinking that a farewell feast ran counter to Christianity, was aghast. "What! my mother, would you have me sin so near to my death?" The mother tried to convince him that it was not a problem, but her efforts were to no avail. At last she brought a Jesuit to his side, who "assured him that in that feast there was no sin."[10] Finally convinced, the boy allowed his mother to stage the farewell feast. The woman invited about a hundred friends to this new, hybrid ritual—a Christian *athataion*. Thus did the Jesuits counter the traditionalists, who mobilized precontact mortuary practices in new ways, by likewise encouraging the use of precontact deathways to new ends. Indeed, Ragueneau allowed other hybrid rituals and dances to help reduce the appeal of traditional Wendat deathways. And even though he never specifically endorsed a Christian Feast of the Dead, Ragueneau's missionary philosophy suggests that he would have embraced such a possibility, just as Brébeuf had in 1636.

But a Christian Feast of the Dead never came to pass. Ragueneau assumed the position of Superior in 1645, during a lull in Iroquois attacks on Wendake. In 1646, however, the Wendats faced the full fury of Iroquoia's well-armed warriors. Simply put, the Senecas had decided to destroy Wendake.

In the early 1640s the Senecas had started to raid Wendake, looking for furs and captives, after their attacks on the St. Lawrence River had not generated as much of either as they had hoped. The forays into Wendake by the Senecas and their Mohawk allies were lucrative, but again an even more attractive option suggested itself: with their growing supply of firearms, the Iroquois would attempt to empty Wendake of its Wendat inhabitants. The Seneca plan was to destroy one village after another, starting in the easternmost reaches of Wendake and moving westward. The Iroquois would capture and adopt as many Wendats as they could, killing or dispersing the rest. Once Wendake was empty, the Senecas could take control of the territory, using it as a base from which to hunt, trade, and launch war parties.

The Senecas put this plan into action with a series of devastating attacks on Wendake in 1646. In response, some Wendats decided they had had enough and fled their homeland altogether. This group, mostly traditionalists, went to live among their Algonquin neighbors to the north. Several longhouses of traditionalists and one Christian family left their kin networks and village cemeteries behind and headed to an easily defended area, surrounded on all sides by lakes and rivers, some five or six days' journey north, where they hoped to escape the Iroquois menace. Harder to elude were the Black Robes. Echon made the treacherous trip to Algonquin territory in order to pray with the Christians and try to convert the others.

Most traditionalists, however, remained in Wendake in an attempt to preserve their way of life. Ironically, their strategy centered on acquiescing to the Iroquois. By 1647 it had become increasingly clear to many traditionalists that they could not stave off the attacks of their better armed enemies. But rather than settle for captivity or dispersal, these traditionalists hoped to accept Iroquois dominion over Wendake in return for being allowed to stay in their homeland. It is unclear exactly how this would have worked in practice, but it likely would have involved the traditionalist Wendats paying tribute in

the form of furs and perhaps captives to their Iroquois overlords. The Wendats would lose their treasured autonomy, but they would retain the ability to
practice Wendat rituals, including the Feast of the Dead, in their homeland.
To some the trade-off made sense.

The key to this new traditionalist strategy was to kill the Jesuits or at least
expel them from Wendake. This would weaken the Christian Wendat faction
and allow the traditionalists eventually to triumph, or so they hoped. With
traditionalists in power, they would be in a position to negotiate a tributary
status with the Iroquois, who were still firmly opposed to Christianity.

The cost of banishing or killing the Jesuits would be high: it would mean
the end of trading with the French, who had long indicated that the Jesuit
presence was a precondition of the alliance. A reduction of European goods
flowing into Wendake would mean not only material hardship for those who
had grown accustomed to the convenience of copper kettles and iron axes,
but also spiritual hardship for traditionalists who had become used to sup-
plying the dead with glass and porcelain beads. The Iroquois might be able to
provide some of these items, in a long trading chain stretching to Dutch Fort
Orange, but not as much as the French. Still, some traditionalists felt that the
sacrifice would be worth it to retain their customs.

So on April 28, 1648, several traditionalist headmen from across Wendake
met to plot their next move. They decided to kill the first Frenchman they
met, hoping to inspire a traditionalist rebellion against the Jesuits. Two Wendat warriors headed for Sainte-Marie, knowing that this was the likeliest spot
to find the French. Sure enough, a short distance outside the mission center's
palisade they came upon twenty-two-year-old Jacques Douart, a servant who
had lived at Sainte-Marie for six years. A hatchet blow killed the young man
instantly.

Douart's bloody corpse communicated an unmistakable message to the
Jesuits. In all the years that the French had been in Wendake, and despite
numerous earlier threats, no French person had ever suffered bodily harm at
the hands of a Wendat. For the first time a Wendat's action left a Frenchman's
clothes stained in blood, not unlike Brébeuf's vision in 1644.

Suddenly "the whole country was in commotion." Christian Wendats,
hearing of the brutal murder, rushed to Sainte-Marie to defend the embattled
Jesuits. The converts declared themselves willing to die to protect the Black
Robes. "I am not afraid of being killed for the Faith," one Christian Wendat declared, "and of giving my life for God, who will make it immortal."[11] If

Wendake descended into civil war, these Christian warriors would be on the front lines of battle.

But it did not happen. The headmen who engineered Douart's murder did their best to whip sympathetic Wendats into a martial frenzy. They sent word that the Jesuits "should be driven from the country." Some of the headmen went even further and stated that Christian Wendats "should be banished from [Wendake], and their number be prevented from increasing."[12] Traditionalists did not, however, rise up across Wendake. Whether because they did not want to jeopardize the French alliance, or because they believed that murder was not the appropriate way to deal with the problem, the hoped-for rebellion never materialized.

This left the traditionalist resurgence broken and demoralized. Moderate traditionalist headmen who were not involved in plotting Douart's murder felt that they had to offer compensation to the French following customary Wendat procedures. This differed from the French punishment for murder, where an individual was held responsible and, if convicted, was executed in a biblical eye-for-an-eye framework. Among the Wendats, by contrast, "it is the public who make reparation for the offenses of individuals," Ragueneau wrote. "In a word, it is the crime that is punished" rather than the murderer himself. Ragueneau found this communal punishment "very efficacious for repressing evil," as had Brébeuf when he had described the practice a decade earlier.[13]

The purpose of the Wendat condolence ritual was to defuse the rage of the murdered person's kin. If the anger remained unaddressed, it could lead to calls for vengeance and possibly war between villages or nations. Douart had no kin in Wendake, and the Wendats weren't really worried that the Jesuits might seek vengeance for his death, but the traditionalists adhered to customary protocols in order to demonstrate their remorse. To do so, they drew upon a metaphorical language that reflected the Wendat reverence for bones.

The headmen of all the Wendat nations invited the Jesuits to a council meeting. With great gravity the leading headman told the Black Robes that Douart's murder threatened to undo the French alliance. "This country is now but a dried skeleton without flesh, without veins, without sinews, and without arteries, like bones that hold together only by a very delicate thread," he declared, referring to the dramatic depopulation of Wendake due to epidemics. "The blow that has fallen upon the head of your nephew," he said, using Wendat kinship terminology to describe Douart's relation to the Jesuits, "has cut that bond." The bones of that skeleton—the French and Wendat allies—now lay scattered across the land. The headman told Ragueneau, "It is for you to collect all those scattered bones."[14] In other words, it was up to the Jesuits to name the price of compensation so the alliance could be restored.

Ragueneau understood the Wendats' idiom of death and bones, so he handed the headman a bundle of one hundred sticks, representing the number of presents the French demanded to pay for Douart's murder. This was on the high end of compensation demands—sixty was the typical number for a murdered man—but the headmen understood that this was an unusually delicate situation and acceded to the request. They returned to their villages to gather the presents.

A few days later they returned and the condolence ritual commenced. Two Christian and two traditionalist headmen led the ceremony. The presents, although they were items of relatively low value such as shells and beads, each carried an important symbolic weight. The first present, for example, was accompanied by the words, "We wipe away your tears by this gift." Its purpose was "so that your sight may be no longer dim when you cast your eyes on this country which has committed the murder." Then followed nine presents to erect a symbolic scaffold grave for the deceased, even though he was a Christian: four gifts representing the four posts holding up the scaffold, four others symbolizing the crossbars, and one to represent the headboard. Next, eight headmen "brought each a present for the eight principal bones in the frame of the human body—the feet, the thighs, the [upper and lower] arms."[15] Other presents metaphorically clothed Douart's dead body and removed the hatchet from his bloody wound. Thus the Wendats used the language of bones and blood and human remains—a grammar the Jesuits well understood—to communicate with their French allies.

This grand and solemn ceremony, which lasted several days and included numerous speeches, was a success from the perspective of the headmen who orchestrated it. The French felt likewise. Brébeuf, Ragueneau, and the rest of the Jesuits accepted the presents in the spirit in which they were given, and in turn they offered presents and speeches attesting to the strength of the alliance. The condolence ritual "succeeded beyond our hopes," according to Ragueneau.[16] The traditionalist resurgence was over.

But a renewed sense of unity between Christian Wendats and moderate traditionalists was not enough to stave off increasingly effective Iroquois attacks. Less than two months after the condolence ritual, hundreds of Iroquois warriors crept undetected into Wendake and laid waste to two villages in the southeastern portion of the country: a small settlement and a large palisaded village, named Teanaostaiaé, with roughly one thousand residents.

The Iroquois, maximizing the element of surprise, attacked Teanaostaiaé just after sunrise on July 3, 1648. Although well defended behind a sturdy palisade, this village was weaker than usual because many men were away fishing or trading. The Iroquois took advantage of this and quickly scaled the palisade after overwhelming the Wendat lookouts. The attackers fired their muskets and wielded their hatchets while bellowing their war cries. Teanaostaiaé soon descended into chaos. In the chapel, where Father Antoine Daniel was performing the morning Mass for a large number of Christian Wendats, people began running to and fro, some to escape the enemies and others to meet them head on. Daniel's reaction was quite different. He dipped his handkerchief into water and baptized the churchgoers by aspersion, sprinkling them in the desperate hope that he could save their souls before the Iroquois killed them.

Fire soon raged everywhere, as the Iroquois put the torch to the longhouses. The attackers headed to the chapel, where they found Daniel and several of the Christians. They quickly killed the Black Robe with a shot from a musket and several arrows. The Iroquois then desecrated his corpse, set fire to the chapel, and threw Daniel's mangled body into the flames. Ragueneau later claimed that Daniel's corpse was "so completely consumed that not even a bone was left."[17] This was almost certainly an exaggeration; it would have required extraordinary temperatures—over 1,500 degrees Fahrenheit—to incinerate the priest's bones. Ragueneau's statement may have been an excuse for why no one had gathered Daniel's holy bones to serve as relics.

Whatever the case, Daniel was the first Jesuit killed in Wendake, a martyr in the eyes of his colleagues. Indeed, Daniel became more than a martyr to his fellow Jesuits; he became a ghostly presence. After his death, during a meeting of the Jesuits, Daniel "was seen to appear in their midst, to revive us all with his strong counsel." The ethereal image "seemed to be about thirty, as far as could be judged by his face."[18] This was strong evidence that Daniel, who had been killed at age forty-eight, was in heaven, as the resurrection of the saints would entail not their mortal bodies with their wounds and imperfections but rather flawless versions of their bodies at roughly thirty years of age. The Jesuits asked the spirit questions and he responded at length.

The Wendats who escaped the destruction of Teanaostaiaé had few such comforting thoughts to ease their pain. About seven hundred of their loved ones—mostly women and children—had been killed or taken captive. Some of those who escaped fled to distant villages. Many others headed to Sainte-Marie. The mission center was fast becoming a refuge to displaced Wendats, with nearly three thousand visitors per year, sometimes as many as six or seven hundred in a span of only two weeks. These refugees did not stay permanently, preferring instead to relocate to new villages, but they sought the protection of Sainte-Marie's stout new stone walls whenever Wendake rang with alarms that the Iroquois were attacking.

The Jesuits welcomed these visitors with a safe place to sleep and three meals a day of *sagamité* seasoned with smoked fish. The priests were especially eager to help converts, but they did not turn away traditionalists, hoping that French largesse would demonstrate Christian generosity—a trait highly valued in Wendake. Attracted to the Black Robes' supernatural power, as well as Sainte-Marie's food, Wendats sought baptism in vastly increased numbers. In 1647, five hundred Wendats were struck with water, and the following year eight hundred more took part in the ritual. In this the Wendats were aided by the Jesuits' relaxed baptismal standards. Where previously the missionaries wanted to make sure that potential converts were well versed in Christian doctrine before baptism, Wendake's state of emergency convinced the Jesuits to baptize all who sought the ritual.

The increasing power of Christian Wendats was evident in villages such as Ossossané, which was home to the oldest mission and such zealous converts as Chiwatenhwa and the first woman to be buried at Sainte-Marie. In 1648 Christians became a majority in Ossossané. Toward the end of that year they held a council meeting in which they selected Ossossané's primary missionary, Father Pierre-Joseph Chaumonot, to be their headman, or "chief of their Captains." Like a traditional Wendat headman, Chaumonot offered advice about which rituals to perform—and which were forbidden. Christian Wendats followed his lead and prevented traditionalists from engaging in a healing ceremony in which young women had sex with a variety of partners. And when a traditionalist had a dream that told him he needed to cut down a tree in which hung a bell used to call the Christians to Mass, an eighty-year-old man prevented him from doing so. This was a stunning departure from traditional norms: "according to the customs of this country," a Jesuit wrote, "it would have been an unheard-of crime to oppose in the least degree the fulfillment of a dream proclaimed so openly."[19] In Ossossané, traditionalists found themselves in an ever-shrinking minority.

Christian Wendats had little time to congratulate themselves on this turn of events. Unknown to them, even as the residents of Ossossané were electing a Black Robe as headman of their village, a force of one thousand Seneca and Mohawk warriors marched inexorably toward Wendake. The Iroquois made this arduous and unprecedented wintertime journey so they could take the Wendats completely by surprise. Before the sun rose on March 16, 1649, the Iroquois descended on the heavily palisaded village of Taenhatentaron. Residents could not believe they were being attacked so early in the year; there weren't even lookouts in the guard towers. The town was taken almost without a fight. Only ten Iroquois died while killing and capturing the four hundred residents of Taenhatentaron.

Three men escaped the carnage. They ran, nearly naked, three miles across the snow to the village the Jesuits called St. Louis. They arrived shouting the news that the Iroquois were attacking. Five hundred women and children and elderly persons fled for their lives, heading for nearby Sainte-Marie. Some eighty Wendat warriors stayed behind to defend their stockaded village. Remaining with them were two Black Robes: Gabriel Lalemant and Jean de Brébeuf.

As day broke, the Iroquois reached St. Louis and immediately began to try to chop through the palisade. With arrows raining down on them, the attackers methodically hacked away at the defenses with their hatchets—likely iron ones obtained from the Dutch. When the hail of arrows became too fearsome, the Iroquois retreated to gather their strength. Once again they tried to chop down the stockade, and once more they were repulsed. But finally the Iroquois breached the palisade and entered the village.

Three miles away in Sainte-Marie, the Jesuits and refugee Wendats could tell what happened next by the smoke that rose from the village. The Iroquois had set fire to the longhouses. What those at Sainte-Marie could not see but could only imagine were the hatchet blows that killed many of the warriors and the gathering of captives for adoption and torture. Among the prisoners were Lalemant and Brébeuf.

The Iroquois stripped the captives naked and forced them to march to Taenhatentaron, the village they had surprised only a few hours earlier. This village they had deliberately not torched so they could use it as a base for further attacks on Wendake—and as a convenient site for the torture of prisoners. As the captive Black Robes and Wendats entered Taenhatentaron, they were greeted with "a hailstorm of blows with sticks upon their shoulders, their loins, their legs, their breasts, their bellies, and their faces."[20] This was but a mild preview of what awaited them.

The captors singled out the Black Robes for the first tortures. Stepping forward to take a lead role in the torments were several Wendat traditionalists, "former captives of the Iroquois, naturalized among them."[21] These men had been taken prisoner in earlier raids on Wendake and, like many others, had become assimilated into Iroquois society. Their gleeful participation in the Jesuits' torture reflected traditionalist rage at the changes ushered into Wendake by Brébeuf and the other Black Robes. Epidemics, death, factionalism, loss of autonomy—all these would be repaid with red-hot awls and hatchets.

It is ironic that Europeans supplied the very items that allowed some groups such as the Iroquois to refine their torture techniques, which in turn were employed on select unlucky Europeans. Iron awls and hatchets became the torture implements of choice for the Iroquois, as they stayed sharp and heated up quickly in a flame. Thus, when Brébeuf attempted to preach to the Christian Wendats who were his fellow prisoners, the Wendat traditionalists among the captors reached for their European iron. They fastened Brébeuf to a post and pierced him with "sharp awls and iron points." Then they put a "necklace" of red-hot hatchets around his neck so he could not avoid their searing heat.[22]

Brébeuf turned to the traditionalist captors and began preaching to them, urging them to accept the word of Christ. This enraged them even more. They tore off Brébeuf's lips to shut him up, "but his blood spoke much more loudly than his lips had done." In other words, his courage, as he stood bloody and tied to the post, impressed the torturers. The captors responded with an unholy version of baptism. Having witnessed the deaths of numerous Wendats struck with water by the Jesuits, the traditionalists turned the tables on Brébeuf, dousing him three times with boiling water. As they poured the scalding water the traditionalists mocked the Black Robe: "Go to heaven," they jeered, "for you are well baptized."[23]

Still, Brébeuf remained stoic through six hours of torture, finally dying at about four o'clock on the afternoon of March 16, Lalemant not long after. Impressed by Brébeuf's display of courage, the captors cut out his heart and ate it, hoping to gain his power by consuming his body and blood. Having journeyed to the New World to teach the Wendats how to die a good Christian death, Echon died a good Wendat death, stoic in torture to the very end.

Torture of Brébeuf. In 1664 an engraver imagined this scene based on the descriptions in the *Jesuit Relations*. The artist emphasized Brébeuf's reported stoicism as his flesh was cut away from his arm and he wore a necklace of red-hot hatchets. Detail of Grégoire Huret, "Preciosa mors quorundam Patrum é Societ. Jesu," in François Du Creux, *Historiae Canadensis*. Photograph © Buffalo and Erie County Historical Society, used by permission.

The Jesuits at Sainte-Marie learned all this from several Christian Wendats who escaped from Taenhatentaron. The following day, after the Iroquois had vacated their temporary stronghold, leaving behind little more than mangled corpses, the Jesuits dispatched shoemaker Christophe Regnaut to recover the human remains. Regnaut found the corpses of Brébeuf and Lalemant, easily identifiable owing to the distinctive wounds they bore, and carried them back to Sainte-Marie.

Because he considered these remains to be the "precious relics" of martyrs who would perhaps one day be saints, Regnaut "examined them at leisure, for more than two hours." He was not content with merely looking at Brébeuf's corpse. Instead, he touched it, as if he were handling the bones of a saint in a reliquary. Regnaut "saw and touched" the blisters caused by the unholy baptism, he "saw and touched" the scars made by the red-hot hatchets, he "saw and touched" where Brébeuf's lips had been ripped off, and he "saw and touched" the opening from which the captors had torn Brébeuf's beating heart. Satisfied that this was indeed Brébeuf, and perhaps feeling blessed by the intimate encounter with a martyr's remains, Regnaut buried the body along with a little lead plaque that read, "Fr. Jean de Brébeuf, burned by the Iroquois, 17 March 1649."[24]

Outside of Sainte-Marie, Wendake was in a state of terror. No one knew where the Iroquois would strike next. To make matters worse, famine stalked the land. March was ordinarily a lean time, as food stores began to run low before the spring runs of pike and sturgeon. This year was leaner than ever, because the threat of Iroquois attacks the previous autumn had resulted in a meager corn harvest. Starving Wendats vainly searched the snowy forests for acorns and edible roots.

Fearing that they might be the next Iroquois target, residents of each village, one after another, abandoned and set fire to their towns, so the Iroquois could not use them as strongholds to stage further attacks. By the end of March all fifteen of the remaining Wendat villages had been reduced to ashes. The Wendat Confederacy was dead.

In desperation many of the roughly seven thousand surviving Wendats headed to Sainte-Marie, where the Black Robes still had abundant food supplies. The Jesuits counted "more than six thousand" refugees at Sainte-Marie, and even if this was an exaggeration, the situation soon became unsustainable.[25] The mission center could serve as a temporary shelter for a large number, but the Jesuits could not keep thousands of hungry bellies filled with *sagamité* for long. Plus, the Jesuits knew that even their robust defenses would not protect them from the Iroquois indefinitely. Hence, they decided to abandon Sainte-Marie.

In early May the Jesuits and their servants began preparing to leave the mission center that Ragueneau called "our second Fatherland, our home of innocent delights."[26] They built a rickety raft and loaded it with as much as it could hold. On May 14 they set fire to the remaining structures so they would not fall into Iroquois hands. With their chapel and dwellings in flames at their backs, the Jesuits paddled their barely seaworthy craft to Gahoendoe, a small island two miles from Wendake in Georgian Bay, where they hoped to reestablish their mission. Despite all that had happened, the Jesuits remained optimistic about converting the Wendats, renaming the place Christian Island.

But before they abandoned Sainte-Marie, there was one more crucial task to accomplish. The Jesuits did not want the Iroquois to desecrate the graves of Brébeuf and Lalemant, so they had Regnaut the shoemaker prepare the corpses for transport to Quebec. In an unwitting mirror of the Feast of the Dead, Regnaut disinterred the bodies, boiled them in strong lye, and scraped any remaining flesh from the bones. He carefully dried the bones in a small clay oven, heating them just a little each day so as not to damage them. When the bones were dry, Regnaut wrapped them in silk and packed them into two small chests. His bone bundles ready, Regnaut carried them to Quebec. There, transformed into relics, Brébeuf's holy bones were "held in great veneration" by the French.[27] There is no evidence, however, that Quebec's Christian Wendats likewise revered Echon's bones.

Epilogue

Bones of Contention, Bones of Consolation

THE WENDAT CONFEDERACY WAS DEAD, but the Wendat people lived on. After 1649 the Wendat diaspora scattered in several different directions. Their numbers were greatly reduced from the twenty-one thousand who lived in Wendake when Samuel de Champlain became the region's first European visitor in 1615. Fewer than one-third remained after the devastating diseases and warfare of subsequent decades. Yet the surviving Wendats, Christians and traditionalists alike, did their best to maintain the beliefs and practices that were most meaningful to them.

Bones continued to be central to their story, as had been the case from the beginning. Bones in particular and deathways more generally had always been crucial elements of Wendat self-definition. For centuries, even before Iroquoians migrated to Wendake, these people's most important ritual had been *Yandatsa*, "the Kettle," what the French would call the Feast of the Dead. In the fourteenth century the Feast symbolized the mingled destinies of a single village's residents, and by the fifteenth century the ossuary represented the ties of amity among the villages that constituted a nation. Simply put,

Wendats believed that nothing was more significant than the proper ritual treatment of human remains.

In the seventeenth century Europeans arrived, including magical Black Robes who likewise believed in the power of holy bones. They carried to Wendake the bones of saints and applied them to sick Wendats and Frenchmen in order to preserve their lives. At first this common ground—a shared belief in the power of human remains—allowed for communication between Jesuits and Wendats. Jean de Brébeuf "admired" the Feast of the Dead, and some Wendats responded favorably to the Jesuits' use of blood and bones in healing rituals. But ultimately Brébeuf did not admire the Feast enough to leave it alone. He used his knowledge about indigenous deathways to try to effect wholesale changes in Wendat religious views.

Brébeuf sincerely believed that Christianizing the Feast and teaching the Wendats about Christ's redeeming blood would save them from an eternity of fiery torments. Nevertheless, his efforts to convince the Wendats that the Feast was "foolish and useless" set in motion a chain of events that helped lead to Wendake's destruction. As Wendats fled for their lives in 1649, they brought with them little more than memories. Some of their most powerful memories were of the human remains that had sanctified Wendake's landscape.

When the Jesuits arrived on Gahoendoe in May 1649, they found thousands of Wendats who had already come to the island seeking shelter from the Iroquois. The Jesuits quickly set about building a new mission center, this one more of a military fort than the palisaded town of Sainte-Marie. The new structure was 120 feet square with a foundation and bastions made of stone and cement. It held the Jesuits and their workmen and the year's supply of corn they had brought from Sainte-Marie. It did not house the Wendats, who had to content themselves with hastily constructed longhouses outside the protection of the fort.

Nonetheless, as word circulated through Wendake in the summer and autumn that the Jesuits were building a defensive fortification on Gahoendoe— and that they had surplus food—even more Wendats got into their canoes and paddled across the choppy waters of Georgian Bay to the island. They encountered a scene that daily grew more desperate. The Wendats who had arrived early enough had tried to plant corn, but the lack of cleared land and a drought that parched the island throughout the summer meant that the harvest was pitifully small. At first the Wendats were able to survive on acorns, but as autumn turned into winter and four feet of snow blanketed the island, even that meager ration disappeared. The Wendats appeared as "dying skeletons eking out a miserable life."[1] Hundreds perished. The living were so weakened that they could not even bury the dead.

In secret some of the survivors began to eat the remains of their deceased relations. "Mothers fed upon their children; brothers on their brothers."[2] Those who were forced into this desperate measure hid their cannibalism because even though Wendats heartily enjoyed the ritual consumption of enemies, they were horrified by the prospect of eating their own people. This was the very antithesis of the respect for the dead that was at the heart of Wendat social and religious norms.

The Jesuits tried to feed the hungry, but they were overwhelmed by the sheer number of refugees. The Jesuits gave the neediest residents copper tokens that could be redeemed for *sagamité* seasoned with a bit of smoked fish. The Wendats who received these handouts were grateful, although they probably could not help noticing that the Jesuits did not starve. The Black Robes felt they had to keep themselves strong so they could baptize the dying and bury the dead.

In the spring of 1650, two old headmen approached Ragueneau. "My brother," one said, "your eyes deceive you when you look upon us; you believe that you see living men, while we are but specters, the souls of the departed." Unless the headmen and the Jesuits took drastic actions immediately, the world as they knew it would be destroyed. "The ground you tread on," they warned Ragueneau, "is about to open under us, to swallow us up, together with yourself, that we may be in the place where we ought to be, among the dead."[3] They revealed that a council of Wendats had met the previous evening and resolved to leave the island. At first the Jesuits did not want to go, hoping against hope that Christian Island could live up to its new name. But after a few days of discussion, the Jesuits agreed that the lack of food and continued fear of the Iroquois rendered the island unfit for a mission center. They would return to Quebec with some of the Christian Wendats.

But which ones? There were thousands on the island who had received baptism, yet the Jesuits felt they could sustain only a fraction of that number on the long journey to Quebec. In the end, roughly three hundred Wendats accompanied the Jesuits to the safety of the French settlement. The rest would have to fend for themselves.

In addition to the group that went to Quebec, the Wendat diaspora fanned out in two different directions. One portion of those who fled Gahoendoe joined with the closely related Tionnontaté Nation (also called the Petun or Tobacco Nation) who lived just to the south of Wendake. Because this group's homeland was also under siege by the Iroquois, the Tionnontatés and the Wendats who joined them fled hundreds of miles northwest to Mackinac Island, famed for its fisheries. Over time these people came to be known as Wyandots, a variation of "Wendats."

Another group, in all likelihood a larger number, sought refuge among the Iroquois. Although at first glance this might appear to be a suicidal strategy, it was based on the belief—well founded, as it turned out—that the Iroquois were eager to assimilate foreigners into their depleted ranks. Indeed, the Wendats who voluntarily joined their former enemies did so at the urging of their relatives who had earlier been captured and adopted by the Iroquois. The two headmen who spoke with Ragueneau told him that some Wendats on Gahoendoe "speak boldly of taking their wives and children, and throwing themselves into the arms of the enemy, among whom they have a great number of relatives who wish for them, and counsel them to make their escape as soon as possible from a desolated country, if they do not wish to perish beneath its ruins."[4]

The Wendats who chose this route faced grueling initiation ceremonies, including being stripped naked and beaten severely, and they endured the dislocation of leaving behind the land where their ancestors' bones lay. But once assimilated into Iroquois society, they were able to continue speaking an Iroquoian language, worshipping a variety of sky and water spirits, and venerating human remains. One thing they could not do, however, was perform a Feast of the Dead. The Iroquois did not use communal ossuaries, and there is no archaeological or documentary evidence that the Wendats naturalized among them were able to introduce the ritual.

Even though their deathways changed, the Wendats in Iroquoia retained memories of life and death in Wendake. And at least some remembered Jean de Brébeuf as an evil sorcerer. In 1669 the Jesuit Etienne Carheil labored among the Cayuga Nation of Iroquois, trying to convert them to Christianity. Carheil came upon a young woman who was dying and hoped to baptize her. When he entered her longhouse, he learned that her father had been a Wendat captive adopted by the Iroquois decades earlier.

Carheil pressed ahead, trying to get the dying woman to accept baptism, but she would not listen to him. Her Wendat father stepped forward to explain her reluctance. "You speak," he said to Carheil, "as formerly Father de Brébeuf used to speak in our country; you teach what he used to teach; and as he used to make people die by pouring water on their heads, you also wish to make us die in the same manner." Carheil was stunned. "I then recognized fully that there was nothing to hope for."[5] A shaman entered the longhouse to perform some healing rituals, and he demanded that Carheil leave. The woman died shortly thereafter without having been struck by water.

Elsewhere, Brébeuf was remembered more positively. Jesuits continued to venerate the founder of the Wendat mission. They also continued to use his bones to cure Indians and demonstrate the healing power of Christianity. Father Henri Nouvel, for example, worked among the Ottawas on the northern coast of Lake Huron in 1672. One of his favorite curatives was a holy potion made by steeping Brébeuf's bones in water. To at least three different patients he administered the magical water. One Ottawa child was so sick that Nouvel "did not think any human remedy could save" him. So Nouvel turned to his supernatural remedy. On three successive days the child drank the water in which Brébeuf's bones had soaked. On the second day "a cure was wrought."[6]

While some of Brébeuf's relics traveled far and wide in the satchels of Jesuit missionaries, other bones remained in Quebec, where they helped cure French colonists of illnesses natural and supernatural. In 1663, for example, a woman who had been possessed by demons for two years was, according to the testimony of a high-ranking Church official, instantly cured when she touched Brébeuf's bones. There are no reports, by contrast, that the Christian Wendats who moved to Quebec in 1650 sought out Brébeuf's bones for their healing powers.[7]

But this was not due to their lack of interest in Christianity. The Wendats who settled in Quebec, as well as the children they bore there, were devout Catholics whose religion was shaped by numerous powerful linkages with precontact practices. This syncretic faith resulted from the many parallels between Catholic and traditional Wendat beliefs, which allowed for the relatively easy interpenetration of the two systems. At the communities of Notre Dame de Foy (est. 1669), Lorette (1673), and Jeune Lorette (1697), bones and deathways remained central to the Christian Wendat understanding of the supernatural world. In 1675, Jesuit Claude Dablon described the hybrid burial practices at Lorette. As soon as a person in the community died, the headman let out "a lugubrious cry through the village to give notice of it."[8] The deceased's kin then dressed the person in his or her finest garments and covered the corpse with an expensive, new red blanket. A priest hurried to the dwelling to pray for the soul of the deceased.

"After that," Dablon wrote, "nothing is done beyond what is customary for the French, until the grave is reached." At that point the prayers and ceremonies that were identical to those of a French Catholic funeral gave way to distinctive Christian Wendat practices. Hearkening back to the precontact funeral feasts at which relatives distributed presents to the dead and to members of the community, families in Lorette displayed their possessions, "from which they give various presents." The first present, usually a "fine large porcelain collar," was offered to the church "in order that prayers may be said for the repose of the dead person's soul." The family next gave gifts to those who buried the deceased and to the dead person's "most intimate friends."[9]

Finally, it came time to bury the body. But instead of placing a shrouded body directly into the earth, as the French did, the Wendats of Lorette did their best to prevent dirt from touching the fully clothed corpse. They created, in effect, an underground scaffold burial. They dug an enormous grave, four or five feet deep and "capable of holding more than six bodies." They lined the bottom and all four sides of the grave with bark. According to Dablon, "this forms a sort of cellar, in which they lay the body." Then, on top of the corpse, the mourners placed a large piece of bark "in the shape of a tomb." The purpose of this tomb-shaped bark covering was to "hold up the earth that is to be thrown on it; the body thus lies therein as in a chamber without touching the earth at all."[10] Over time the flesh would slowly decompose and leave dry bones, as if the person had been buried on a scaffold. The bones would not, however, be gathered into a communal ossuary.

After the burial the mourners returned to Lorette's church, where everyone took communion "for the repose of [the deceased's] soul," consuming Christ's body and blood in order to remember their Savior's sacrifice that ensured eternal life for believers. "The chief object" of these combined French and Wendat practices, according to Dablon, was to "place [the deceased] on the road to heaven."[11] No longer did these Wendat souls travel to Aataentsic's village to the west.

Several days after this hybrid funeral, it was time for another feast. This ceremony served to bring "the deceased back to life," or, as Dablon hastened to explain to skeptical readers, "that is, to give his name to another, whom they urge to imitate the dead man's good actions while taking his name."[12] Whereas precontact Wendats had believed that the souls of the dead could be reanimated in newborns, the Christians of Lorette maintained a symbolic version of that tradition by having the deceased's name continue with the living.

This connection between the living and the dead also explains why the Catholic feast of All Souls' Day (November 2) was attended with such devotion in Lorette. On this day of commemoration Catholics pray for the souls of all the dead, including the deceased who do not have living relatives to pray for them, in an effort to get the souls out of purgatory and into heaven. According to Dablon, as soon as the bells began to ring on All Souls' Day, reminding people to pray for the deceased, "our chapel was filled with people, and it was not empty until a late hour on the next day." Lorette's Wendats remembered the dead so zealously that "we were obliged to leave our church open throughout the night, to satisfy their devotion."[13]

All Souls' Day remained central to the worship of Wendat Christians even after the move to Jeune Lorette in 1697. The Jesuit Louis d'Avaugour wrote in 1710 that as October ended and All Souls' Day drew near, hunters who had been in the woods pursuing beavers returned to Jeune Lorette "to attend the divine mysteries." The men and women of the community offered "pious prayers" to the "souls of the dead, a duty which they perform with remarkable piety and attention."[14]

Meanwhile, the branch of the Wendat diaspora that joined with the Tionnontatés and became known as Wyandots endured dislocations far beyond what the Lorette Christians faced. Despite their long journey to Mackinac Island in 1650, they still felt vulnerable to the Iroquois, so they traveled to present-day Wisconsin and then west to the Mississippi River. There they encountered the powerful Sioux, who pushed them all the way back to Mackinac in 1671. The French encouraged the Wyandots to move to Detroit, which they did in 1701. In the 1740s, the Wyandots relocated to Sandusky, Ohio, hoping for greater autonomy. There they claimed sovereignty over a large portion of what is now Ohio. Joined by Delawares and Shawnees in the 1750s, the Wyandots regained some of their earlier power and influence, but ultimately they could not fend off the land hunger of Euro-Americans. In 1795 they were among the numerous native groups that signed the Treaty of Green-ville, which gave most of Ohio to the United States.

President Andrew Jackson's Indian Removal Act of 1830 foreshadowed fur-ther relocations. In 1843 the U.S. government removed nearly seven hundred Wyandots from their reservations in Ohio and Michigan to a new reserva-tion in Kansas. This forced departure was especially painful because it meant leaving behind nearly a century's worth of ancestors' bones in the Sandusky cemetery. As the Wyandots prepared to leave, their leader Squire Grey Eyes offered a poignant speech. "Here our dead are buried," he said to his people. "We have placed fresh flowers upon their graves for the last time. No longer shall we visit them. Soon they shall be forgotten, for the onward march of the strong White Man will not turn aside for the Indian graves."[15]

Even in Kansas the Wyandots were not long protected from the "onward march" of Euro-Americans, who once again lusted for their land. In the 1860s and 1870s some Wyandots sought refuge in Indian Territory (which later be-came Oklahoma). There they were eventually recognized by the U.S. gov-ernment as the Wyandotte Tribe of Oklahoma. Others remained in Kansas, where they jealously guarded the Wyandot Cemetery against encroachment, as it lay on valuable real estate in Kansas City. Ironically, one of the great-est threats to the cemetery came from Oklahoma's Wyandottes, who in 1899 hoped to move the human remains and sell the land to developers. This pat-tern was repeated throughout the twentieth century, as the Oklahoma Wyan-dottes tried on several occasions to sell the Kansas cemetery. This occurred most recently in the 1990s, when the Oklahoma Wyandottes hoped to build a casino on the land. Tensions between the Oklahoma and Kansas descendants of the Wendats reached the breaking point.

Fittingly, bones brought them back together—not the contentious remains in Kansas City, but the bones from Ossossané where Jean de Brébeuf had wit-nessed the Feast of the Dead in 1636. Ever since the Ossossané ossuary had been excavated by Royal Ontario Museum archaeologists in the 1940s, the remains had traveled from one research center to another, where Euro-Amer-ican scientists studied, measured, and catalogued them. In 1974, a Wendat boy named Michel Gros-Louis visited Ossossané with his father. Gros-Louis hailed from Lorette, now called the Wendake Reserve, a place where even to-day 94 percent of residents are Catholic and a powerful sense of Wendat iden-tity persists.[16] In Ossossané Gros-Louis read the roadside historical marker at the site of the 1636 Feast of the Dead and learned, to his horror, that his ancestors' remains were stored in the ROM. The young Gros-Louis promised his father he would someday rectify the situation.

By the end of the twentieth century the political climate surrounding indigenous human remains had changed sufficiently that Gros-Louis finally had a chance to keep his promise. In 1990 the U.S. Congress passed the Native American Graves Protection and Repatriation Act (NAGPRA), which gave American Indians the right to sue for the return of human remains and grave goods held in museums and private collections. Although this law did not apply north of the border, Canadian museum curators were sensitive to the same concerns that led to the passage of the U.S. law. In 1999, after consulting with lawyers, the ROM agreed to return the Feast of the Dead bones to Ossossané.

Thus, the four branches of the Wendat diaspora—the Huron-Wendat Nation of Wendake, the Wyandottes of Oklahoma, the Wyandots of Kansas, and the Anderdon Wyandots of Michigan—decided they needed a ceremony of reconciliation in advance of the repatriation of bones. They wanted to resolve the tensions that had arisen among them in the previous centuries, so the bones could be reburied in a spirit of harmony. For the site of the reconciliation ceremony they settled on Midland, Ontario, in the heart of the Wendat homeland—a place locals still call Huronia, as can be witnessed on signs for the Huronia Martial Arts Academy and the Huronia Denture Clinic.

Midland is also a crucial location for those who venerate the bones of Jean de Brébeuf. It is the home of the Martyrs' Shrine, a Catholic church built in 1925 to memorialize the seven Jesuits, including Brébeuf, killed while trying to Christianize the Wendats and Iroquois in the seventeenth century. Catholic officials overseeing the construction of the church wanted Jesuit relics at the Shrine, so they moved several bones from Quebec, including part of Charles Garnier's leg, Gabriel Lalemant's rib, and, most dramatically, half of Brébeuf's skull. The Shrine obtained this last cherished item from the generous Ursuline nuns of Quebec, who held the complete original. According to a booklet available at the Shrine, Brébeuf's skull "was sawed in two vertically through the middle of the face in such a way that the Jesuits and the Ursulines could expose both sides for public veneration, once a facsimile of the missing side was completed in wax."[17] With the relics in place, Brébeuf and the other Jesuits were canonized by Pope Pius XI in 1930.

Today St. Jean de Brébeuf's skull peers out from an ornate reliquary, the centerpiece of devotion for the thousands of Catholics who annually make pilgrimages to the Shrine. During the daily Mass, the priest invites people forward, where he offers prayers for each individual. The priest intones, "Through the prayers of God's holy martyrs, may the Lord bless you and protect you all the days of your life, may you remain in health in mind and body."[18] As he speaks these words, he presses against each worshipper's forehead slivers of Brébeuf's bones, encased in a doorknob-shaped glass and brass reliquary. In death Brébeuf continues his work as a healer among believers and skeptics in Wendake.

A very different set of bones and memories motivated the members of the Wendat diaspora who gathered in Midland in June 1999 for the reconciliation ceremony. In preparation for the reburial of the Ossossané remains, the various Wendat factions met for three days and apologized to one another for their differences and their lack of communication over the years. The Wyandottes of Oklahoma apologized to the Wyandots of Kansas for the cemetery conflict. In turn, the Kansas Wyandots said they were sorry for the hurtful words they had spoken during the controversy. Chief Leaford Bearskin of the Oklahoma Wyandottes shook the hand of Kansas Wyandot Cultural Coordinator Darren Zane English—a man who also goes by the name Chiwatenhwa—and said simply, "you are Wyandot."[19] All four Wendat groups also received apologies from representatives of the Catholic Church.

The path was now cleared for the solemn business of reburying the bones held by the Royal Ontario Museum. On August 29, 1999, 350 years after the death of the Wendat Confederacy, the four branches of the Wendat diaspora gathered at dawn for what they described as a new Feast of the Dead. The mingling of their ancestors' bones would once again symbolize the ties that bound them despite their geographic dispersal. Several hundred descendants of the Wendats awaited a truck carrying acid-free museum boxes filled with bones. In the cool air they stood on the very spot where Brébeuf watched the 1636 Feast, and like Brébeuf they were astonished by the size of the burial pit, ten feet deep and sixty feet across, although this ossuary had been dug with a diesel backhoe rather than wooden spades.

Finally the truck arrived. The participants knew there would be a lot of boxes, but they were nonetheless taken aback when the truck opened to reveal three hundred boxes arranged in stack upon stack. Wendat descendants, including Francis Gros-Louis, a member of the Huron-Wendat Nation who lived in Virginia, began to unload the truck: "Fourth in line I waited my turn. As my turn came I felt totally traumatized as I walked up the steel ramp into

Brébeuf's Skull. This ornate reliquary at the Martyrs' Shrine displays bone fragments from Gabriel Lalemant and Charles Garnier, but Brébeuf's skull holds pride of place. Thousands of pilgrims visit the Shrine annually to see the relics and pray to St. Jean de Brébeuf and the other Jesuit martyrs. Photograph by the author.

the truck and stared down at the box before me. I know that my eyes glistened and blurred with slowly forming tears and my heart beat faster as I stooped to pick up the first of many boxes I carried."[20]

As the sun climbed higher in the sky, the air warmed. Men and women carried box after box to the edge of the pit. In the background several drums beat softly while participants began a rhythmic funeral chant, "Hi, hi, hi, hi." Elders purified the boxes with the smoke of sweetgrass as others carried them to the edge of the pit. At last the truck was empty. It was time to return the bones to the ossuary where they had been placed in 1636.

A human chain formed, with boxes passed from hand to hand and into the pit, the bottom of which was lined with beaver pelts. Michel Gros-Louis, keeping the promise he made years earlier to his now deceased father, stood in the pit and deposited the first items, grave goods that the ROM archaeologists had found during their excavations: copper kettles and shell beads, evidence of the mixed European-Wendat material culture of the original Feast. Madeline Gros-Louis, the ninety-year-old aunt of Michel Gros-Louis and the oldest attendee, then blessed the boxes. "Absolute silence fell over the gathering as the opening of the first box of human remains almost emotionally overwhelmed the three Huron-Wendat in the bottom of the reburial pit."[21] The first box was gently tipped and emptied, revealing leg bones and arm bones and ribs. People gasped as another box containing skulls was emptied onto the growing pile. A raptor rose in the sky; some thought it was a hawk, others a golden eagle, a bird of rich symbolic and spiritual significance.

The repetition of emptying boxes and drumming and chanting brought participants into a trancelike state of communion with their ancestors. As Francis Gros-Louis put it, "my mind cleared and I tried to comprehend my emotional feelings and the thought that perhaps I was carrying the remains of my own Gros-Louis ancestors who had been buried at this site some 350 years ago."[22] After three hours, all the boxes were empty. A circular pile of human remains some six feet deep lay in the center of the ossuary. Several Wendat descendants hoisted shovels and covered the bones with sand. The new Feast of the Dead was over.

A few miles away in the Martyrs' Shrine, Jean de Brébeuf's skull stared out from its reliquary. But this day belonged to the Wendats.

ACKNOWLEDGMENTS

Numerous friends, colleagues, and institutions helped me as I researched and wrote this book. For providing me with a semester off during the initial stage of writing, I am grateful for the fellowship I received from the Humanities Institute at the University at Buffalo. My research assistants, Chuck Lipp and Michelle LaVoie, helped me many years ago in ways that remain valuable to this day. John Steckley, Liana Vardi, and Gary Warrick offered their expertise in response to my questions. Allan Greer read the chapter from *Death in the New World* upon which this book expands; he pushed me to think hard about the sources I use to tell this story. April Hawkins and Mima Kapches in the Royal Ontario Museum's Department of New World Archaeology kindly facilitated my research there. Mima was especially generous in answering my follow-up questions via e-mail and in sharing her unpublished work on the Ossossané repatriation. Bob Brugger at the Johns Hopkins University Press and Peter Hoffer helped steer the book toward publication. Thanks to all.

Several individuals deserve special notice. Neal Salisbury read my book proposal and offered several crucial pieces of advice that helped me get off to a good start. He then read the whole manuscript and suggested revisions that made this a better, more balanced book. I am deeply indebted to him. I benefited from expertise of a different variety from John Motoviloff, a novelist, essayist, and dear friend for thirty years. John also read the whole manuscript and offered valuable advice about clarity and character development. I hope I can reciprocate for his help with the book; I know I can never repay what our decades of friendship have meant. Finally, Victoria Wolcott, my life partner, deserves the deepest thanks of all. She read and commented on all the chapters as I wrote them, patiently listened as I talked at dinner about torture and decomposition, and, most importantly, kept me happy and balanced as I worked on the book. I am pleased to be forever in her debt.

NOTES

Prologue: Encounters with Bones and Death

1. Reuben Gold Thwaites, ed., *The Jesuit Relations and Allied Documents*, 73 vols. (Cleveland, 1896–1901), 10:293 (admired), 10:279 (magnificent), hereafter cited as JR. Allan Greer, ed., *The Jesuit Relations: Natives and Missionaries in Seventeenth-Century North America* (Boston, 2000), 66 (heartening). I prefer Greer's translation of the original "*Il y a du contentement de voir*" as "it is heartening to see" to the Thwaites version's "it is very interesting to see." JR 10:290, 291.

2. Gabriel Sagard, *The Long Journey to the Country of the Hurons*, ed. George M. Wrong (Toronto, 1939), 226.

CHAPTER ONE: The Origins of Wendake

1. JR 33:225.

2. John L. Steckley, ed., *De Religione: Telling the Seventeenth-Century Jesuit Story in Huron to the Iroquois* (Norman, OK, 2004), 31.

3. Population and number of villages from Gary Warrick, *A Population History of the Huron-Petun, A.D. 500–1650* (New York, 2008), 223. The Bog People or Swamp-Dwellers joined the confederacy in 1640.

4. Sagard, *Long Journey*, 171.

5. JR 10:159, 161.

6. JR 17:155–59.

7. John L. Steckley, *Words of the Huron* (Waterloo, ON, 2007), 186.

8. Sagard, *Long Journey*, 206.

9. Ibid., 205.

10. JR 10:267–69.

11. Sagard, *Long Journey*, 208, names and object added to quotation.

CHAPTER TWO: Catholicism and Colonization

1. John Bossy, *Christianity in the West, 1400–1700* (New York, 1985), 14; Edward Muir, *Ritual in Early Modern Europe*, 2nd ed. (New York, 2005), 26.

2. Peter Brown, *The Cult of the Saints: Its Rise and Function in Latin Christianity* (Chicago, 1981), chap. 4.

3. Anthony Pagden, *Lords of All the World: Ideologies of Empire in Spain, Britain, and France, c. 1500–c. 1800* (New Haven, 1995), 33.

4. Laurence Brockliss and Colin Jones, *The Medical World of Early Modern France* (Oxford, 1997), 78.

5. Norman P. Tanner, ed., *Decrees of the Ecumenical Councils*, 2 vols. (London, 1990), 2:710.

6. Jacqueline Thibaut-Payen, *Les morts, l'église et l'état: Recherches d'histoire administrative sur la sépulture et les cimetiéres dans le ressort du parlement de Paris aux XVIIe et XVIIIe siècles* (Paris, 1977), 89–90.

7. George E. Ganss, ed., *Ignatius of Loyola: The Spiritual Exercises and Selected Works* (New York, 1991), 138.

8. A. Lynn Martin, *The Jesuit Mind: The Mentality of an Elite in Early Modern France* (Ithaca, 1988), 183.

9. René Latourelle, *Jean de Brébeuf's Writings: A Study*, trans. William Lonc and George Topp (Midland, ON, 2001), 299.

CHAPTER THREE: First Encounters

1. W. C. Noble, "The Sopher Celt: An Indicator of Early Protohistoric Trade in Huronia," *Ontario Archaeology* 16 (1971): 42.

2. Sagard, *Long Journey*, 79.

3. H. P. Biggar, ed., *The Works of Samuel de Champlain*, 6 vols. (Toronto, 1922–1936), 2:70.

4. Ibid., 2:99.

5. Ibid., 3:45, 47, 162.

6. Sagard, *Long Journey*, 90, 139, 136.

7. Ibid., 75.

8. Ibid., 213.

9. R. Po-Chia Hsia, *The World of Catholic Renewal, 1540–1770*, 2nd ed. (New York, 2005), 210.

10. For the pun on Brébeuf's name, see Joseph P. Donnelly, *Jean de Brébeuf* (Chicago, 1975), 11.

11. JR 3:195, 8:103.

12. Steckley, ed., *De Religione*, 87.

13. JR 10:43–49.

14. The Wendat name for Brébeuf was actually "Hechon," but as the French do not aspirate an initial "h" they rendered it "Echon," which I follow here. Steckley, *Words of the Huron*, 236. On the Wendat construction *aesken de iskiacarratas*, see Steckley, ed., *De Religione*, 32.

15. JR 8:89.

16. JR 8:129–31.

17. JR 8:169.

18. JR 8:137; Steckley, ed., *De Religione*, 153.

19. JR 8:137–39.

20. JR 8:137.

21. JR 8:137.

22. Philip T. Weller, ed., *The Roman Ritual in Latin and English with Rubrics and Planechant Notation*, 3 vols. (Milwaukee, 1950), 2:5.

23. JR 8:145.

24. JR 10:31.

25. JR 10:29.

26. JR 15:81.

27. JR 10:289.

CHAPTER FOUR: The Feast of the Dead

1. Sagard, *Long Journey*, 213–14.

2. JR 10:281.

3. Sagard, *Long Journey*, 211.

4. JR 10:263.

5. JR 10:309.

6. JR 10:305.

7. JR 10:283.

8. JR 10:283.

9. JR 10:297.

10. JR 10:285.

11. Brébeuf never mentioned the date of May 10, but he stated that the Feast was scheduled for the Saturday of Pentecost. In 1636 Easter was March 23, and Pentecost is always seven Sundays after Easter, which puts it that year on May 11. Saturday of Pentecost was therefore May 10. JR 13:251 indicates that the latter part of May was planting time. On the Wendat word for the month of May, see Steckley, *Words of the Huron*, 114.

12. Kenneth E. Kidd, "The Excavation and Historical Identification of a Huron Ossuary," *American Antiquity* 18 (April 1953): 359.

13. Ibid., 364.

14. JR 10:293.

15. Brown, *Cult of the Saints*, chap. 4.

16. Joyce Marshall, ed., *Word from New France: The Selected Letters of Marie de l'Incarnation* (Toronto, 1967), 299–300.

17. JR 10:73.

18. JR 10:303–5.

19. JR 10:295.

20. JR 10:295.

21. JR 10:295.

22. JR 10:297.
23. JR 10:299.
24. JR 10:299.
25. JR 10:301.
26. JR 10:299.

CHAPTER FIVE: Epidemic Tensions

1. Warrick, *Population History*, 224. I have extrapolated the number of Wendat deaths from an estimated population of twenty thousand after the epidemic of 1634.
2. JR 13:95.
3. JR 13:95.
4. JR 13:101.
5. JR 12:69–71; Sagard, *Long Journey*, 193, 197.
6. JR 10:199. In the last quotation I have used the translation in Lucien Campeau, *Huron Relations for 1636 and 1637*, trans. William Lonc (Midland, ON, 2000), 168. Thwaites translates "*guerissez nous donc*" as the more awkward, "Do you cure us, then." JR 10:199.
7. Weller, ed., *Roman Ritual*, 1:339–41.
8. JR 13:99.
9. Steckley, ed., *De Religione*, 11; JR 15:33, 12:237.
10. JR 13:101, 103. His name is usually rendered "Tonneraouanont" in French.
11. JR 13:105–7.
12. JR 13:107.
13. JR 13:103–5.
14. JR 13:105.
15. JR 13:131.
16. JR 13:203; Sagard, *Long Journey*, 197.
17. JR 13:205.
18. JR 13:131–33.
19. JR 13:251.
20. JR 13:207–9.
21. JR 13:151–53.
22. JR 13:227–29.
23. JR 13:231–33.
24. JR 13:241.
25. JR 13:259.
26. JR 14:51, 53.
27. JR 14:53.
28. JR 15:41.
29. JR 15:41, 43, 45.
30. JR 15:47.
31. Latourelle, *Jean de Brébeuf's Writings*, 300.

32. JR 15:63.
33. JR 15:67.
34. JR 14:103.
35. JR 15:91.
36. JR 15:99.
37. JR 15:79, 19:245.
38. JR 19:141, 155, 159.
39. JR 19:251.
40. JR 19:161, 251.
41. JR 19:253, 143.
42. JR 20:79.
43. Latourelle, *Jean de Brébeuf's Writings*, 309.

CHAPTER SIX: Conversion and Conflict

1. JR 26:263.
2. JR 20:27–29.
3. JR 15:93.
4. JR 26:207–9.
5. JR 26:209.
6. JR 26:289.
7. JR 19:91, 241.
8. JR 21:209–11.
9. J. Franklin Jameson, ed., *Narratives of New Netherland, 1609–1664* (New York, 1909), 303. The quotation is from 1649.
10. JR 24:297.
11. JR 26:177.
12. JR 26:177.
13. JR 23:51.
14. JR 23:129–31.
15. JR 26:221; Sagard, *Long Journey*, 197.
16. JR 23:61, 26:205.
17. JR 28:79.
18. JR 23:31.
19. JR 23:213.
20. JR 23:217, 219.
21. JR 24:271.
22. JR 23:135.
23. JR 26:279, 23:135.
24. JR 29:275.
25. JR 29:277.
26. JR 30:23.

CHAPTER SEVEN: Destruction

1. Latourelle, *Jean de Brébeuf's Writings*, 305–6.
2. Ibid., 313.
3. JR 30:25–27.
4. JR 30:27.
5. JR 30:29.
6. JR 30:31.
7. JR 30:31.
8. JR 33:145.
9. JR 33:145.
10. JR 34:113.
11. JR 33:231, 233.
12. JR 33:231.
13. JR 33:235.
14. JR 33:235–37.
15. JR 33:241–43.
16. JR 33:249.
17. JR 33:263.
18. JR 33:267.
19. JR 34:105, 107–9.
20. JR 34:141.
21. JR 34:141.
22. JR 34:143.
23. JR 34:143, 29.
24. JR 34:33–35. The plaque, found by archaeologists in 1954, is on display at Sainte-Marie among the Hurons, Midland, Ontario. It reads, "P. Jean de Brebeuf bruslé par les Iroquois le 17 de mars l'an 1649."
25. JR 34:199.
26. JR 35:83.
27. JR 34:35.

Epilogue: Bones of Contention, Bones of Consolation

1. JR 35:89.
2. JR 35:89.
3. JR 35:191.
4. JR 35:193.
5. JR 52:187.
6. JR 56:103.
7. Quebec's Christian Algonquins reportedly held Brébeuf's memory in "extreme veneration." On one occasion, according to the Jesuits, an Algonquin man was cured by touching Brébeuf's bones. JR 50:123.

8. *JR* 60:35.

9. *JR* 60:35.

10. *JR* 60:35–37.

11. *JR* 60:39.

12. *JR* 60:37.

13. *JR* 60:39.

14. *JR* 66:153.

15. "Farewell to a Beloved Land," http://www.wyandot.org/farewell.htm, viewed September 7, 2009.

16. 2001 Census, Statistics Canada, http://www12.statcan.ca/english/Profil01/CP01/Details/Page.cfm?Lang=E&Geo1=CSD&Code1=2423802&Geo2=PR&Code2=24&Data=Count&SearchText=Wendake&SearchType=Begins&SearchPR=24&B1=All&Custom=, viewed September 9, 2009.

17. Adrien Pouliot, *The Holy Martyrs of Canada*, trans. George Topp (n.p., n.d.), 23.

18. Observation, September 17, 2005.

19. Darren Zane English, "Another Perspective on the Reconciliation in Midland, Ontario," http://www.wyandot.org/reconcil.htm, viewed September 7, 2009.

20. Francis Gros-Louis, "The Reburial of the Human Remains of My 350 Year Old Ancestors," http://www.agondachia.com/cemetery.html, viewed September 8, 2009.

21. Ibid.

22. Ibid.

SUGGESTED FURTHER READING

Primary sources about the Wendat-French encounter are readily available in English. As the notes indicate, this book relies most heavily on the seventy-three-volume edition of the *Jesuit Relations* published at the end of the nineteenth century: Reuben Gold Thwaites, ed., *The Jesuit Relations and Allied Documents*, 73 vols. (Cleveland, 1896–1901). This version includes the French originals and English translations on facing pages. The Thwaites edition is also online at www.puffin.creighton.edu/jesuit/relations and through various databases owned by university libraries. I have found the database "Early Encounters in North America" especially helpful. Other key primary sources include H. P. Biggar, ed., *The Works of Samuel de Champlain*, 6 vols. (Toronto, 1922–1936); and Gabriel Sagard, *The Long Journey to the Country of the Hurons*, ed. George M. Wrong (Toronto, 1939). For extraordinary insights about the Wendats based on their language, see two books by John L. Steckley: *De Religione: Telling the Seventeenth-Century Jesuit Story in Huron to the Iroquois* (Norman, OK, 2004); and *Words of the Huron* (Waterloo, ON, 2007).

The best history of the Wendats is undoubtedly Bruce G. Trigger, *The Children of Aataentsic: A History of the Huron People to 1660* (Montreal, 1976). Trigger's book, with its exhaustive research in literary and archaeological sources, is the standard against which all others are measured. Another important work is Gary Warrick, *A Population History of the Huron-Petun, A.D. 500–1650* (New York, 2008), which focuses on Wendat demographics over a very long period of time. I have relied heavily on Warrick when discussing population figures and disease.

Other helpful overviews include Georges E. Sioui, *Huron-Wendat: The Heritage of the Circle*, trans. Jane Brierley (East Lansing, MI, 1999), which is written by a member of the Huron-Wendat Nation and provides a native perspective on the period; Conrad Heidenreich, *Huronia: A History and Geography of the Huron Indians, 1600–1650* (Toronto, 1971), which takes a geographical approach to its subject and includes a great deal of useful information about Wendake's physical environment; and Elisabeth Tooker, *An Ethnography of the Huron Indians, 1615–1649* (Washington, DC, 1964), which is especially helpful for its extensive citations of primary source material. If one looks up the section on "Feasts," for example, one is immediately led to the key passages in the *Jesuit Relations*. Joseph P. Donnelly's *Jean de Brébeuf* (Chicago, 1975) is a well-written biography, but it suffers from the author's hagiographic approach to his subject.

There has been a great deal of important archaeological work done in Wendake. Trigger and Warrick extensively cite and evaluate this literature. The key source on the excavation of the Ossossané ossuary is Kenneth E. Kidd, "The Excavation and Historical Identification of a Huron Ossuary," *American Antiquity* 18 (April 1953): 359–79. The human remains from Ossossané are analyzed in M. Anne Katzenberg and Randy White, "A Paleodemographic Analysis of the *Os Coxae* from Ossossané Ossuary," *Canadian Review of Physical Anthropology* 1 (1979): 10–28. An important collection of essays on the history and archaeology of Iroquoian ossuary burials is Ronald F. Williamson and Susan Pfeiffer, eds., *Bones of the Ancestors: The Archaeology and Osteobiology of the Moatfield Ossuary* (Gatineau, QC, 2003).

Kidd performed the first professional excavations at Sainte-Marie among the Hurons and published his findings in *The Excavation of Ste Marie I* (Toronto, 1949). Wilfrid Jury then completed the dig and wrote *Sainte-Marie among the Hurons* (Toronto, 1954). This book was geared toward an audience beyond professional archaeologists; it therefore does not include the detailed data specialists expect. Indeed, there are serious problems with some of Jury's interpretations, as explained in Jeanie Tummon and W. Barry Gray, eds., *Before and Beyond Sainte-Marie: 1987–1990 Excavations at the Sainte-Marie among the Hurons Site Complex (circa 1200–1990)* (Dundas, ON, 1995).

Several historians have placed Wendat history in the context of wider French and Indian interactions in Canada. Karen Anderson's *Chain Her by One Foot: The Subjugation of Native Women in Seventeenth-Century New France* (New York, 1991) offers a provocative if somewhat simplistic argument about how the adoption of Christianity oppressed indigenous women. Carole Blackburn's *Harvest of Souls: The Jesuit Missions and Colonialism in North America, 1632–1650* (Montreal, 2000) emphasizes Indian resistance to French teachings. John Webster Grant's *Moon of Wintertime: Missionaries and the Indians of Canada in Encounter since 1534* (Toronto, 1984) offers nuanced analyses of native encounters with missionaries in Canada over a long time period. Denys Delage's *Bitter Feast: Amerindians and Europeans in Northeastern North America, 1600–64*, trans. Jane Brierley (Vancouver, 1993), pays deserved attention to the material and geopolitical context of the story. The two best books on the Iroquois expansion into Wendake are Daniel K. Richter, *The Ordeal of the Longhouse: The Peoples of the Iroquois League in the Era of European Colonization* (Chapel Hill, 1992); and Jon W. Parmenter, *The Edge of the Woods: Iroquoia, 1534–1701* (East Lansing, MI, 2010).

Pulling back the lens even more, there are several important books on native-missionary encounters in northeastern North America that have decisively shaped my interpretations. James Axtell's classic *The Invasion Within: The Contest of Cultures in Colonial North America* (New York, 1985) compares and contrasts the Jesuits with Puritan missionaries in New England. Axtell's book is analytically powerful and a great read. The same combination can be found in Allan Greer, *Mohawk Saint: Catherine Tekakwitha and the Jesuits* (New York, 2005). As a distinguished historian of the early modern French Atlantic, Greer is more attentive than most to the religious and ideological context of the Jesuit mission. Emma Anderson's *The Betrayal of Faith: The*

Tragic Journey of a Native Convert (Cambridge, MA, 2007) is an extremely well-written account of one Innu (Montagnais) man's encounter with the Jesuits.

Two other recent books offer subtle readings of native encounters with Christianity: David J. Silverman, *Faith and Boundaries: Colonists, Christianity, and Community among the Wampanoag Indians of Martha's Vineyard, 1600–1871* (New York, 2005); and Rachel Wheeler, *To Live upon Hope: Mohicans and Missionaries in the Eighteenth-Century Northeast* (Ithaca, 2008). My own analysis of interactions throughout eastern North America and the Caribbean may be found in Erik R. Seeman, *Death in the New World: Cross-Cultural Encounters, 1492–1800* (Philadelphia, 2010).

To learn more about the European religious context of the Jesuits who came to North America, the following overviews are good starting points: John Bossy, *Christianity in the West, 1400–1700* (New York, 1985); and R. Po-Chia Hsia, *The World of Catholic Renewal, 1540–1770*, 2nd ed. (New York, 2005). Books more focused on the Jesuits include John W. O'Malley, *The First Jesuits* (Cambridge, MA, 1993); and A. Lynn Martin, *The Jesuit Mind: The Mentality of an Elite in Early Modern France* (Ithaca, 1988). Two useful surveys of disease and medicine in early modern Europe are Laurence Brockliss and Colin Jones, *The Medical World of Early Modern France* (Oxford, 1997); and Mary Lindemann, *Medicine and Society in Early Modern Europe* (New York, 1999).

European deathways are the subject of Philippe Ariès's sweeping *The Hour of Our Death*, trans. Helen Weaver (New York, 1981). Because Ariès examines deathways in all of Europe through two millennia, his work tends toward overgeneralizations. More specialized and more reliable works include Peter Brown, *The Cult of the Saints: Its Rise and Function in Latin Christianity* (Chicago, 1981), about the origins of Catholic veneration of human remains; Patrick J. Geary, *Living with the Dead in the Middle Ages* (Ithaca, 1994), on the encounter between Christian and non-Christian deathways in central and northern Europe; and Vanessa Harding, *The Dead and the Living in Paris and London, 1500–1670* (Cambridge, UK, 2002), a work whose comparative approach allows one to see what was distinctive about early modern French deathways.

And for something completely different, order *Black Robe* from Netflix. This 1991 film is not a dry documentary but rather a dramatic Hollywood imagining of interactions between native peoples and the French in Canada. The title character, loosely based on Jean de Brébeuf, journeys with Algonquin guides from Quebec to Wendake. Cross-cultural understandings and misunderstandings—some centering on deathways—drive the plot.

INDEX

Oquiaendis, 54
original sin, 25–26
origin stories: Christian, 24–25; Wendat, 6–8
Ossossané, 1–2, 62, 91, 120, 127, 140–41
ossuaries, 60–61, 67–78, 140–44
Ottawas, 137

palisades, 11, 128
Paraguay, 102
Paré, Ambroise, 31
plague. *See* bubonic plague
Pope, 27, 36, 141
population figures, 10–11, 80, 92, 99, 106, 131, 133, 150n1
post molds, 69–70
prayers, 48, 51–52, 78, 82, 87; of European Catholics, 26–27, 30–34, 36; of Christian Wendats, 97, 114, 138
Protestant Reformation, 24, 28–29
psalms, 33, 78
purgatory, 26, 35, 43, 139
Puritans, 44

Quebec, 40, 48, 50, 116, 132, 135–38, 141

Ragueneau, Paul, 120–21, 124–26, 131, 135
Récollets, 41–44
Regnaut, Christophe, 130–32
reincarnation, 65, 119, 139
relics, 74–75, 126, 131–34, 141–43; of Brébeuf, 131–32, 137, 141–44; in Europe, 27, 31; in Wendake, 75, 98–99
reliquaries, 27, 31, 34, 98, 131, 141–44
Requiem Mass, 33
resurrection, 111–12, 121
Ridley, Frank, 68, 70
rings, 71, 73
Rock Nation, 11, 38, 39, 41
Roman Ritual, 55
rosary beads, 105–6, 114
Royal Ontario Museum (ROM), 67–69, 74, 140–42, 144

sagamité (corn porridge), 12, 19, 67, 127, 135
Sagard, Gabriel, 4, 5, 42, 45, 83, 111; on Feast of the Dead, 43, 61, 62
Sainte-Marie among the Hurons, 102–6,

116–20, 123, 127–28, 131–34; archaeology of, 105–6; and Christian Wendat burials, 104–5, 119; construction of, 102
saints, 92, 97–99, 141; in Europe, 27, 31
Sandusky, Ohio, 139–40
Satan, 24, 26, 27, 53, 87
scaffold burial, 20–22, 91, 112, 115, 138
Senecas, 107–10, 122, 128
servants, 49, 64, 76, 83, 102, 123
sexuality, 42, 47, 127
shamans, 17, 47–48, 85–88, 90–91, 110, 137
shrouds, 33–34, 65
Sioux, 139
sky, 20, 91, 100–101; worship of, 8, 13, 136
smallpox, 14, 30, 50–51, 107; symptoms of, 106
Society of Jesus. *See* Jesuits
Sopher Celt, 38–39
souls, 2, 14–16, 42–43, 65, 119–20; Christian belief in, 26–27, 52, 111, 139; Wendat belief in, 7–9, 12–13, 20, 88
Squire Grey Eyes, 140
St. Lawrence River, 40, 48, 107–8, 122
St. Louis, 128
strep, 80–81
sun, 7–8, 120; worship of, 13
Swamp-Dwellers. *See* Bog Nation
sweat lodges, 16, 87, 110
sweat ritual, 16, 86–87, 97, 110
syncretism, 105–6, 137–38

Taenhatentaron, 128, 130
Tawiscaron, 7–8
Teanaostaiaé, 126
Tehorenhaegnon, 47–48, 91
Tionnontatés, 136
Toanché, 45–50
tobacco, 11, 13, 87, 102
Tonnerawanont, 85–88, 90
torture, 18, 25, 128–30
Totiri, Etienne, 100–101, 114–15
trade goods, 3, 38, 95, 107, 123; in Feast of the Dead, 39, 60–61, 74–76; in scaffold burials, 22; spiritual power of, 4
traditionalists, 99–101, 107, 110, 112–16, 118–25, 127, 129; definition of word, 99; derision of Christians, 112, 114; visions of, 101, 119–20